MW01015655

To Where the MOEI RIVER *Flows*

by LENA ADAMS

with Paula Montgomery

WESTBOW
PRESS®
A DIVISION OF THOMAS NELSON
& ZONDERVAN

WestBow Press books may be ordered through booksellers or by contacting:

WestBow Press
A Division of Thomas Nelson & Zondervan
1663 Liberty Drive
Bloomington, IN 47403
www.westbowpress.com
844-714-3454

Because of the dynamic nature of the Internet, any web addresses or links contained in this book may have changed since publication and may no longer be valid. The views expressed in this work are solely those of the author and do not necessarily reflect the views of the publisher, and the publisher hereby disclaims any responsibility for them.

Any people depicted in stock imagery provided by Getty Images are models, and such images are being used for illustrative purposes only. Certain stock imagery © Getty Images.

Some names of people in this book have been changed.

Cover photo by Josiah Adams
Chapter 19, personal insert by Emily Crosman. Used by permission.

Unless otherwise indicated, all Scripture taken from the New American Standard Bible (NASB) Copyright ©1960, 1962, 1963, 1968, 1971, 1972, 1973, 1975, 1977, 1995 by The Lockman Foundation, La Habra, CA. All rights reserved. Used by Permission. www.lockman.org.

Scripture marked (ICB) taken from the International Children's Bible®. Copyright © 1986, 1988, 1999 by Thomas Nelson. Used by permission. All rights reserved.

Scripture marked (NKJV) taken from the New King James Version®. Copyright © 1982 by Thomas Nelson. Used by permission. All rights reserved.

Scripture marked (KJV) taken from the King James Version of the Bible.

ISBN: 978-1-6642-1625-9 (sc)
ISBN: 978-1-6642-1624-2 (hc)
ISBN: 978-1-6642-1626-6 (e)

Library of Congress Control Number: 2020924682

Print information available on the last page.

WestBow Press rev. date: 01/08/2021

CONTENTS

PART 4: THAT THEY MIGHT BE CALLED TREES OF RIGHTEOUSNESS

PART 5: THE PLANTING OF THE LORD

PART 6: THAT HE MIGHT BE GLORIFIED

To my children,
Emily, Maria, Anna, and Josiah,
and to my husband Paul,
I dedicate this book especially to you,
because without a complaint,
each of you has sacrificed so much
in order for our family to live out God's love and truth
before those He has called us to serve.
With deep gratitude, I also dedicate this book
to those who have partnered with us
through their prayers and giving,
thus enabling this ministry
to continue to feed the hungry,
clothe the naked,
and spread God's love and truth.

1

Beauty for Ashes

CHAPTER 1

Escape from Lay Klo Yaw

The Burmese army's coming!" our oldest daughter Emily exclaimed over the crackling phone. "We're evacuating the younger children at first light, and I'm staying behind to look after them until they're all across the river with you."

When Emily insisted on staying until all the younger children in the mission school had crossed the Moei River to our side of the border, my mind whirled with the realization that none of us could hesitate, not even to consider the consequences. We knew those by heart, and the dark thoughts chilled me to the bone despite Thailand's tropical heat and humidity that permeated everything inside our wooden house.

A good friend, Eh K'Nyaw, worked at the Lay Klo Yaw mission school on the other side of the river in Karen State, Burma. Occasionally, he would mention hearing that the Burmese army was coming. But then those rumors faded along with any worries. A little before Christmas, word spread again that we could expect the dreaded army at any time to overrun the mission school. But to our great relief, that prediction didn't materialize either.

Now it was June, and the rainy season was just beginning its annual debut with sporadic downpours that turned most trails and roads to mud. Consequently, the faculty at the school relaxed, thinking an attack would happen only during the dry season. Nevertheless, some preparations remained in case the Burmese threat came true.

When 20-year-old Emily had accepted a teaching position at Lay Klo Yaw, crossing the river from Thailand into Karen State just the evening before, she was well aware of the dangers. In fact, because of those dangers, she waited until dusk to load her belongings and herself into a canoe. Emily realized her height, long blond hair, and fair skin would make an easy target for an enemy soldier, but fear found no place in the excitement she felt. Our daughter was eager to follow God to another corner of the world where some special Karen children needed her—and Him.

The river she had crossed was no longer the clear, serene water that, only a few weeks before, had mirrored the pyramid-shaped mountains standing like tall sentinels on the Burma side. The rains were intensifying, muddying the Moei, thus preventing reflections of any kind in its cocoa-colored waters.

Stepping into her new role, Emily helped the youngsters prepare to leave. Older girls and women, who normally appeared calm, now cried as they yanked still-damp laundry off bamboo poles. They all knew their fate if left in the path of the brutal army. Some recalled deeply buried events from their own experiences, having watched mother, sister, or aunt savagely violated, tortured, and killed. Those who hadn't actually witnessed such scenes had heard the horrific reports while gathered around evening fires.

When I shared Emily's evacuation news with my husband Paul and asked how we would manage so many children, he calmly looked at me and quoted Jesus' words in Mark 10:14: *"Let the little children come to Me, and do not forbid them; for of such is the kingdom of God'" (NKJV)*. That quote became Paul's pat answer whenever we heard future rumors of more children heading our way.

My husband then shuffled outdoors to make sure our "Old Trusty Rusty" crew-cab truck was ready for its part in hauling children, teachers, and other staff. At three inches over six-feet tall,

Paul must have looked like a giant to the small Karen students and even to the teenagers and adults. But since we had arrived at our mission post in Thailand seven months earlier, we—along with our four children—had crossed the Moei River several times to attend special events at Lay Klo Yaw. The most recent event was Eh K'Nyaw's wedding when he married lovely Eh Do Say, a shy, but sweet Christian teacher at the school. Furthermore, our second-oldest daughter Maria had taught at Lay Klo Yaw part of the school year before. So the students and staff were already familiar with my Herculean-sized husband, whose strong arms could easily help anyone trying to scramble up the slippery banks to safety on the Thailand side of the Moei.

And Paul did just that. Beginning at dawn over the next few days, he carefully loaded small groups from the canoe landing to the truck bed of Old Trusty Rusty. Then, time and again, my husband would maneuver the truck through deep ruts in a neglected banana patch and onto the overgrown, muddy trail that led to the winding two-lane road toward our property.

Wherever we were during that evacuation, many of us silently prayed for God to slow the Burmese army, allowing all the children and staff to escape in time. We prayed, too, that He would muffle the noise of the motor attached to the canoe transporting everyone—and for the safety of the passengers as the canoe plowed through waters where deep currents held stray logs and debris that could easily topple a boat.

In the meantime, I stayed busy pounding nails and hooks into the rustic walls and ceiling throughout our house; then I strung lines for mosquito nets. On the other side of the river, Emily was packing those nets into children's bags, so everyone would be protected at nightfall from the disease-bearing insects and their pesky stings. Our daughter also packed a large number of sleeping mats.

On that initial day of the evacuation, I gladly welcomed a few teachers and the school cook, all carrying oversized pots and other supplies for boiling rice upon large rocks that would encircle fires in our yard. Just the sight of those women instantly eased my anxiety about preparing enough food for so many people.

Paul made seven trips that first day until those adults and seventy of the youngest children arrived on our side of the river without incident. That night about an hour after supper and worship with our many houseguests, I gazed around at all the nets, some in white and others in various shades of orange, pink, and blue. The multi-hued nets covered the few adults and the scores of exhausted little ones as their sleeping bodies filled nearly every inch of our 600-square-foot home. Finding no room inside for Paul and me, we strung our oversized net on the front porch and lay our wide sleeping mat on the wooden boards. The plastic, braided mats offered no physical comfort, but our spirits were soaring with gratitude to God for safely delivering this first round of evacuees.

Paul took a few moments then to describe how our friend Eh K'Nyaw had herded groups of terrified youngsters from the school dormitories down to the river where he helped them and their baggage into the waiting canoe. Eh K'Nyaw was a great asset to the children. Not only had he graduated from a Christian seminary with a degree in theology, but he was also fluent in Karen, Burmese, and even English!

Some of those students were orphans, but the others came from such poverty that living at the school had provided their only way to survive. And trying to return to their homes would have meant dealing with freshly laid landmines, likely starvation, or equally dangerous, the Burmese army.

My husband couldn't actually hear Eh K'Nyaw's soft voice so far away, but he guessed the man was speaking soothing words to those youngsters in the process of being uprooted from their beloved school and the only real security they had ever known. Now they toted bulging baggage over their small shoulders. And by the time the children had splashed through muddy puddles down to the waiting canoe, Paul witnessed a dramatic change. He said he could see (across the river) that many of them were smiling, and their voices had taken on gleeful sounds as they chatted back and forth. He and I both agreed that Eh K'Nyaw was most likely behind their transformation. The man was, indeed, a true asset—and a gifted servant of God. And now with his bride, they made an inspiring team.

Next, my husband mentioned the older boys who were helping as well. Each time the canoe left, those brave young men would stand on the Burma shore, bidding the youngsters goodbye. Paul could hear their strong voices calling across the river, "See you in the morning!" My husband said he detected an extra fervor in those voices, as if the teenagers were trying to cover any semblance of fear by sounding overly cheerful.

Despite fleeing often from the enemy during the decades-long civil war in Burma, the Karen people were known for their joy and great sense of humor even under such severe circumstances. And those brave young Karen men, standing at the river's edge that day, were fine examples.

"Please, Father, take care of the others left at Lay Klo Yaw tonight, including our daughter Emily," I prayed aloud as droning mosquitoes and croaking frogs sang a lopsided lullaby with our sleepy "Amen!"

While Emily stayed behind during that first day and night, doing her best to encourage the remaining children and women, there beat a heart for adventure within our daughter. Perhaps that yen for adventure was born during her childhood while living in a Montana forest that our family shared with enormous grizzly bears. Once, when little Emily lost sight of a grizzly wandering near our sturdy cabin, she tearfully pleaded with me to allow her to go outside and chase after the bear, so she could see it up close! Now, although beyond weary, Emily felt adrenaline of the same sort coursing through her veins, boosting her energy as she continued to help people, small and large, in their escape from Lay Klo Yaw.

I also felt adrenaline coursing through my veins the next morning when I awoke to the faint sounds of artillery fire way off in the distance. My thoughts, of course, rushed immediately to Emily, who was still at the school.

Father, please, keep your powerful, protecting angels round about my sweet daughter and the rest of your people remaining at Lay Klo Yaw!

Others had apparently heard the same sounds of war, because Paul witnessed how nearby villages were literally emptying as frightened people fled to the Thai highlands. And in just hours, those villages were mostly deserted. Likewise, the Moei had become quite busy as more and more Karen civilians were finding ways to cross the rough waters and also flee to hills and mountains on our side of the river. With most of the neighboring villages empty, except for a few sick or crippled people who were unable to flee with other inhabitants, Paul and Old Trusty Rusty weren't needed during those few days for their usual ministry—that of transporting patients to hospitals—and thus, he and our truck were available exclusively for transporting the Lay Klo Yaw school refugees. To my overwhelming joy, our daughter Emily was one of those refugees that day. (And I probably embarrassed her with my enthusiastic hugs and vocal praises to God for His mighty power and mercy.)

On the third day of the evacuation, with machine gunfire and larger explosions growing louder, the final load of teenage boys (most carrying rescued textbooks and other school supplies), along with Eh K'Nyaw, left the Burma shore just in time before the dreaded army arrived.

Almost immediately, enemy soldiers set fire to the school, destroying its buildings. Our hearts ached at the sight of black smoke billowing up from the direction of Lay Klo Yaw.

At odds with my grief, however, was an overwhelming gratitude for God's miraculous deliverance. All 120 children and the school staff were safely across the border on our side of the river.

I couldn't help but consider a few of the verses from Exodus 15's song of Moses and the children of Israel. Surely, our joy-filled hearts at least somewhat echoed the praises of the Israelites when God delivered them from the pursuing Pharaoh and his army: "*The*

Lord is my strength and song, And He has become my salvation; This is my God, and I will praise Him; My father's God, and I will extol Him. . . . In Your lovingkindness You have led the people whom You have redeemed; In Your strength You have guided them to Your holy habitation" (Exodus 15:2, 13).

Then, quite unexpectedly, my joy was transformed into wonder as I glanced around at the many youngsters of various sizes inside our house, those outside, dangling their legs over the edge of our front porch, and others taking advantage of a lull in the rain by frolicking in the muddy yard. Even with loud explosions across the river, shaking the very ground at their feet, those youngsters still played! Neither loud mortars nor mud could dampen their sweet Karen spirits. In that moment, I couldn't help but feel an all-consuming love for those little ones. And I suddenly understood our daughter's stubborn desire to stay with every last one of those younger students until they were all safely on our side of the Moei.

But, Father, whatever shall we do with all these precious children?

CHAPTER 2

Faith Journey

As our house and porch on the Thai-Burma border overflowed with ten-dozen Karen children and additional adults during those first war-torn days, I realized how radically our lives had changed. Not too many months before, our family had decided to devote "just one year to missionary service" in a country other than ours in North America. My own life had certainly veered off in an unexpected direction compared to my upbringing in Sweden, a land of castles, cathedrals, cobblestone streets, and endless lakes.

I recall once during those early years, asking a sincere and solemn question, "*Mamma*, is there a God?"

To her abrupt "No," tears trickled down my face. What had seemed a plausible possibility on my part began to wash away with those tears. And eventually, I came to accept that there was no God, which meant a childhood without faith, without prayer.

What I considered Sweden's "cathedrals" were actually majestic-looking Apostolic Lutheran Churches that my family visited just on special occasions, such as weddings and funerals. With the only noise my echoing footsteps, the few times I entered those serene sanctuaries alone were to admire their architecture and ornate beauty. During one of those times, I noticed some women, stooped with age, lighting candles near the front. I subsequently came to view Christianity as an "old woman's religion."

During those Sweden years, my dear mother often worked long hours to provide for us children. My one grandmother, *Farmor*, an artist, did her best to teach my brothers and me proper etiquette with "visiting" manners. She had lived in a quaint, seaside cottage in a small village. *Farmor's* mother, my great-grandmother, lived in a castle where *Farmor* spent her youth. We children would visit our great-grandmother's castle from time to time, but we favored Farmor's seaside cottage. Our other grandmother, *Marmor*, who lived closer, was deeply involved in our everyday lives and lavish with her love for us.

During my late teens, I launched upon a personal quest to become "pure" and could find no inherent power within myself to accomplish such a goal. On the other hand, by following the ways of the world, I also found myself constantly fighting a battle with appetite. Magazine models always looked so slender. And in my effort to follow suit, I became obsessed with dieting—and developed an eating disorder.

When my mother discovered my destructive behavior, she sent me to a counselor. But I felt even more helpless when I realized that nothing that professional could say changed my obsession.

I then started a frantic search for meaning in life, and that quest eventually took me to faraway lands (like Calcutta, India) where I observed the Hindu, Buddhist, and other ideologies in person. As those belief systems proved empty to me—vain rituals with no satisfying answers—I became desperate in my search. Even drawn to Mother Teresa, who gave her all to suffering humanity, I still faced a huge void in my life.

One night when sleep wouldn't come, I cried, "God, are You there?" Then I screamed in misery—not an audible scream, but an intense soul cry. What happened next remains vivid in my memory. I felt an invisible hand upon me. It was a forceful, yet tender, sign that seemed supernatural. I could finally allow myself to believe that a Supernatural Being did exist. But who was this Being? I still didn't know Him, but I felt certain He knew me. And His ears were open to my cry, even a cry no human could hear.

In those days my custom was to spend evenings, reading some interesting book by candlelight, often a book from an Eastern philosophical perspective. Meanwhile, I sipped tea sweetened with a spoonful of honey, savoring those moments of quiet reflection.

One evening while settling down for my special time with yet another book, to my dismay, there was absolutely nothing to read that appealed to my hungering spirit. So I turned to the bookshelf in the furnished apartment where I lived a short distance from the outskirts of Stockholm. That shelf had never drawn my interest before, because its books abounded in unfamiliar topics. After finding nothing that appealed to me, I glanced at a tattered Bible.

"Should I read it?" I wondered. "No, it's just for old women." Arguing with myself a little longer, I reluctantly took the Bible off the shelf, sat down, then started to read. I was surprised to find the Old Testament accounts quite interesting. Today, I realize it was my theological ignorance that suddenly caught me in a philosophical bog that memorable evening. And I nearly dismissed the Bible altogether. Instead, I peeked into the New Testament, which started me on a journey through the stories about Jesus.

Reading verse after verse, I noticed tiny references to other texts regarding a similar word or subject in the Bible. I began to look up each of those texts, and as I studied them, God revealed Himself to me—and faith was born within my very being. To my astonishment, the day arrived when I answered with a resounding "Yes!" such questions as, *Did Jesus walk on water? Was He born of a virgin? Was Jesus both God and man?*

Before I could truly experience the joy that only Jesus offers, however, I felt a deep need for repentance. How I wept as I tried out my new faith in God to forgive me and to make things right in each area of my life that didn't reflect His perfect and loving character!

The greatest wonder that thoroughly thrilled me was the healing from my eating disorder. I had discovered a new power, *God's* power! For those fighting similar disorders, I want to make this clear: although instant deliverance was mine regarding the bulimic behavior and other moral and behavioral struggles in the future, I had to learn to make a *choice*. Then God would supply the *strength* to carry out that choice. I also learned that not all victories are won overnight. Some healing might take years. But as I kept *surrendering* the battle to my Savior, He delivered me according to *His* timetable.

I can now look back and understand why God allowed me to pass through certain trials. He was teaching me to become obedient and humble and to keep looking to Him for help. And during that process He began to reshape my life inside and out. Had He allowed more difficulties to befall me all at once, I surely would have given up. In those early days of my newfound faith, the Lord doled out "learning experiences" bit by bit as I could take them, preparing me for the future.

Next, and most likely not by chance, an elderly "retired" Christian evangelist, named Erik, came into my life. I thought it oddly ironic that he was a longtime friend of my atheistic grandmother who had scoffed at me for even reading the Bible.

One day I received a phone call from Erik. "Please come and visit me," he said, "so we can study the Bible together."

Destitute of any Christian friends or relatives, I was excited by Erik's invitation. Until then, I'd been exclusively alone with Jesus and His Word during my faith journey.

Crossing a bridge in Stockholm's suburbs, I strolled to the nearest station of the *tunnelbana* (subway). There I boarded for my ride downtown. Then I walked to Erik's building and took the tiny elevator to his floor. A bit nervous, I breathed a quick prayer, and knocked on the door.

The elderly gentleman, who was bent over and leaning on a cane, greeted me. His eyes were as blue as a Swedish summer sky. After a hearty welcome, he led me into his small apartment kitchen where the table was set with a delicious vegetarian meal he had cooked from scratch: a hazelnut loaf, mashed potatoes, homemade graham rolls, and orange juice.

This was the beginning of a unique friendship as each week I would repeat the trip on the *tunnelbana*, then take the elevator to Erik's floor. He always had the same vegetarian meal ready; and after dining together, we would retire to the living room (or sometimes stay at the kitchen table) where a large worn Bible always waited nearby. Erik would open the Book with great reverence, and I quickly realized the man knew the Scriptures exceptionally well. With every question I asked, he would flip through the pages and find the exact texts I needed—even for passages I found mysterious.

"How can that be?" I'd exclaim, often questioning the subjects Erik presented.

With an abundance of patience, the man would lean back in his chair and fold his huge hands, smile, and say, "Go home and study on your own, asking God to lead you each step of the way!"

Upon arriving at my apartment, I'd sit down (now with a new Bible, a concordance, a Bible commentary, and a book that covered the most common Christian faiths and their doctrines); then I would search for scriptural answers to my questions. Interestingly, Erik never mentioned a word about any particular Christian denomination.

After quite some time into these intensive lessons, I finally announced, "I want to get baptized."

Looking puzzled, he asked, "How did you arrive at that conclusion?"

"From studying the Bible. . . ." I told him.

A few weeks later I was immersed in the watery "grave" of baptism, then welcomed wholeheartedly by a small Christian congregation in Stockholm. One particular man shook my hand, then whispered in my ear, "Remember, don't look at people, but keep looking at Jesus!"

I wish I could say I followed that stranger's advice every moment from then on, but I cannot. Perhaps I was susceptible to falling in love with someone who didn't believe as I did, because although raised an atheist, I was now enthralled with God's presence in my life. Experiencing an intense joy that only He can give, I reasoned that the American man I met would surely learn how real and wonderful God is.

And so I left my beloved Sweden and settled with my new husband in America's Pacific Northwest. It was there I would eventually give birth to our daughters: first, Emily, then three years later, Maria. At that time, my husband began to build a house perched high above the wide Columbia River with vistas of snowcapped Mount Hood and Mount Adams.

Now my grown daughter Emily stood at my side, helping with the many children who had escaped from Lay Klo Yaw. Her sister, Maria, who taught that school's kindergartners months before, was back in the United States. I knew that Maria's love for our Karen neighbors remained strong and that she looked forward to returning to them with fresh training as an emergency medical technician (EMT), to help with the Karen people's dire health needs.

Meanwhile, Paul and I were facing dire *housing* needs as our small home and porch swelled with way too many people . . .

CHAPTER 3

A Mountain Refuge

First in a succession of miracles, a sympathetic neighbor temporarily opened his lime orchard for some of the children and staff. In the midst of those fruit trees stood an old building, which offered shelter from the frequent downpours so characteristic of Thailand's ongoing rainy season.

Next, we knew that our landlady happened to own a rustic "retreat center" about a 45-minute drive up the mountain that began its ascent behind our house. A beautiful property with a creek, the center's main building came with a large kitchen, several bedrooms, and—best of all—a roomy fellowship area! There were two good-sized cabins, one we could use for a boys' dormitory and the other for the girls.

When Paul and I asked our landlady if we could rent her retreat center for 120 children, she initially declined. And we couldn't blame her. After all, so many young people meant high risk of damage to the facilities. But later, she changed her mind and was even willing for us to keep all the children, teachers, and other staff there. What an answer to prayer!

We decided not to rent this mountain refuge with donated money, but instead, dipped into Paul's retirement savings for that purpose. We also compared the $45 per 24-hour day our landlady charged for the retreat center to what most travelers sometimes paid for one night in a hotel room to accommodate just one or two people. With our boarders numbering about 135, we considered our rent for the center quite reasonable (and nothing short of miraculous).

A few weeks before the evacuation, my husband and I had been puzzled by how the Lay Klo Yaw school and its ministry kept intruding in our usual prayers.

"Paul," I said, "every time I pray—and even during the night—I hear God telling me that we're to become leaders of the Lay Klo Yaw school!"

He surprised me with, "I know."

"But we are not leaders," I exclaimed. "And I don't want to live over there. It makes me afraid."

Then literally overnight, the 120 Lay Klo Yaw children arrived on our side of the river and became dependent on us for everything: housing, food, clothing, medical needs, and their education. Thus, we humbly realized God had brought us to that very place for that very purpose. It was as if He said, "See, I brought the school over the river to you! Now, care for My children faithfully and tenderly."

Despite our inadequacies, whatever God planned for us, we knew He would be our Pilot and Provider for the work. For that reason, we didn't even consider separating the children at that time. And no way would we send them back into the war zone. Their joyful singing and sincere prayers had gripped our hearts as they trusted in God's care and, now, also in ours.

Although we moved the school up to the mountain retreat, staff and all, Paul and I with our two younger children, Anna and Josiah, stayed down at our house. In addition to taking needy people to hospitals in Mae Sot and even to more distant hospitals, my husband and I regularly traveled with supplies up to the makeshift school. The students were in good hands with Eh K'Nyaw and the rest of the staff, which included our Emily who was teaching math and English to third-through-sixth graders.

Meanwhile, the war lingered over the border-river with daily shooting and shelling. The ground would often vibrate along with the booming of explosions. Those continued daily for a couple of weeks. And despite the chaos, Paul still kept busy driving supplies up to the retreat center; he also transported people to hospitals (sick villagers who had stayed behind).

During those few weeks of war, our Anna was recovering from a serious virus. Lying on the floor, she could hear the nearby warfare, but didn't seem alarmed by it. On the other hand, our youngest, Josiah, was easily upset by the thundering artillery. So we made a game of it all when I would challenge him, "Josiah, count the bullets!"

At one such time, I had to swallow a chuckle when he replied, "Mama, I've counted forty. Do you think that's enough?"

Many a morning as Paul would leave at 6 a.m. to transport supplies or people or both, I wished we could join him just to get away from the unrelenting noise; but because of Anna's illness, we needed to stay home.

Meanwhile, officials from the Adventist Development and Relief Agency (ADRA) arrived on scene and saw how the school was still thriving—but on our side of the Moei River. Apparently satisfied with how Paul and I were keeping the former Lay Klo Yaw school functioning, they asked if we would take on its directorship. With Eh K'Nyaw as the "Administrator," we agreed.

Soon thereafter, our young American friend, Dan (who had acted as a one-person welcoming committee when we first arrived in Thailand) suddenly popped back into our lives when he returned from furlough. On this occasion he arrived with two of his brothers in tow—Gabe and Rick.

Gabe left shortly for Cambodia, while Dan asked me to teach Rick the basics of getting around. Then like a flash, Dan was gone again! But his brother Rick remained and became a treasured addition to our lives with his cheerful, mischievous personality. He shared our small home, sleeping on a traditional floor mat as the rest of us did.

One morning, not too long after Lay Klo Yaw school's evacuation, Rick roused me from sleep with a whispered, "I'm going!"

"You're going *where* at 3:30 a.m.?"

"I have to get to the Gloh Mee Taw school before daylight to give them some money," he said. (Gloh Mee Taw was a smaller mission school farther north across the Moei River in Karen State, Burma.)

Rick returned around 9 a.m., pale and stifling tears. "The Burmese have attacked the school! The children are gone, and a man is dead."

CHAPTER 4

The Sending of a Substitute

Shortly after Rick's return to our place, we learned that late the previous night the principal of the small Gloh Mee Taw school had received a warning that a Burmese attack was imminent. Our hearts swelled with praises to God, because despite the darkness and dangerous river, the children had been able to evacuate their boarding school and reach Thai soil—and they were all safe! A few workers and a teacher, however, had stayed behind. Sadly, the teacher was mortally wounded, and the others were taken as porters. (But, later, those captives managed to escape.)

We learned also that Rick had arrived about 4 a.m. at the Moei. While surveying the dark, churning waters before diving in for an early morning swim across to Karen State, Burma, he quickly surmised that the swollen river undoubtedly contained too much debris for him to swim safely across. He knew his only hope was a canoe if he wanted to accomplish his mission before dawn. So our friend hiked to the nearest town to awaken a grandmother associated with the Gloh Mee Taw mission school. While there, Rick found someone nearby with a canoe. Upon returning to the riverbank with the borrowed boat, he heard gunfire. It was apparent to him that soldiers were shooting from Thai soil, together with Burmese soldiers on the other side.

Someone had spotted Rick earlier on the riverbank and concluded that the young American had swum over to Karen State. Because of that siting, a rumor spread that he had been caught in the crossfire; but the rumor was cut short when he turned up, unharmed.

Also, more good news soon reached our ears. The principal of the small Gloh Mee Taw school had a close relative who owned mountain property far north of us; so those children not only found shelter, but also a new site for their school!

Back in earlier days when we first lived in our house on the border, while Maria taught at Lay Klo Yaw and Emily served at a mountain mission post, Paul, the two younger children, and I lived a very simple life. We tried to preserve the local culture and not needlessly erect barriers between the villagers and ourselves. Our tall stature and light coloring were already intimidating; and at every turn we often heard the word, *"gallowah." Gallowah* meant "white person," and we were the first light-skinned people to reside permanently in that area. Today, white people come and go. But back then, the only other American was a missionary friend, who had attempted to keep a low profile on Thai soil, not wanting to draw attention to himself.

Although we lived in a wooden house rather than a bamboo hut at that time, we did sleep on the floor atop plastic mats, customarily used for that purpose. We also ate our meals while sitting on those mats. And our only luxury was a two-burner propane stove. During those early days in Thailand, we were prone to frequent illnesses as well.

Lord, if we shall live like this, will You, please, make us more useful?

Not long after that prayer, a young man named Mowae from a Christian high school in Chiang Mai, asked if he could stay with us during his school break. He was planning to enter medical training to become a physician—"to bless my people," he said.

Of course, he could stay with us! And we enjoyed Mowae, who had spent his childhood at an orphanage in another province. As he grew older, he was trained to transport sick villagers to hospitals.

Moreover, the young man was fluent in English, Thai, Karen—and Burmese!

While walking with Josiah and Anna one evening, Mowae was approached by villagers who invited them to visit in a home. As the threesome entered the house, they met a sick young man who needed to undergo surgery. That sick man became our first patient, followed by thousands over the years, patients treated locally or whom we drove to hospitals farther away for diagnosis, treatment, and surgeries.

Our new friend Mowae miraculously paved the way for that transport ministry by driving to Thai checkpoints and securing permission to transport sick people through their gates. This was extremely important, because anyone who didn't hold Thai identity papers could be taken to the border and transferred to the Burmese authorities.

With God's leading, we vowed to do all we could to help our destitute neighbors and stand by them at checkpoints and at hospitals where, sadly, our village friends were sometimes snubbed or mistreated.

Each time we appeared in a town to transport someone, others also needing medical attention would surround us. We became so busy driving to hospitals that often our only food was doing our heavenly Father's work. Several round-trips a day were not uncommon. We would return weary after four hours on the road (not counting the time spent in a hospital) only to find another emergency. This became a joy-filled labor of love.

There were times when at least one of us in the family would need to stay with a patient in a hospital overnight or longer. When I entered one of those hospitals for the first time, I confess to feeling uncomfortable. To the populace I was a "foreigner," so I drew stares and comments. Only the doctors spoke English. Thus, communication with others could become exasperating. They looked at me with curiosity, probably wondering what I was doing in the hospital—with *their* people. Staying in a ward with a patient day and night was another matter. When I first entered a ward, the stench and heat could cause instant nausea. (But later, I became used to the smells.)

I was surprised at the grime in local hospital wards. A janitor would come around with a broom and sweep the middle of the floor and then mop with a large dirty towel. I never saw or smelled any kind of disinfectant or cleaning solutions. The mopping was done in the same casual way as the sweeping. Blood and body fluids were treated with a nonchalance that was astounding.

On one occasion, after staying a longer time than usual with a patient in the hospital, I came to relax and started to enjoy the diversity. I found myself fascinated by the multitudes and felt privileged to have a "ringside seat" in this hodgepodge of so many cultures together. Inside the crowded children's ward that overflowed out into the hallways, I watched the patients' relatives or friends tend the sick; often entire families stayed with a patient. The caregiver is supposed to do the work as a nurse's aide. That meant assisting in everything except such duties as distributing medicines, giving shots, drawing blood, and hooking up IVs.

There were Burmese Indian Muslims in their long white tunics and prayer caps. One elderly gentleman, in particular, captured my interest. He sported a lengthy gray beard and was dressed in white except for darker long pants underneath. And atop his head perched an ornate prayer cap.

Also in that hospital were Burmese men dressed in their lounges and Burmese women in tasteful tailored skirts and blouses. Karen men and women wore their traditional fringed outfits, with some of the men also wearing lounges. The Hmong dressed in satin black clothing with amazing colorful embroidery. Then there were the Thai's trendy clothes. And last, there were our family's Western and Karen styles.

How interesting to witness this mingling of diverse cultures when sicknesses—and, sometimes, death—brought people together who otherwise wouldn't even think of associating with one another!

Back then we were required to return yearly to the United States for our visa renewals. And several months before the warfare broke out, we had already made plans for the trip (or "furlough"). But now, because of our deep involvement with the evacuated school children, the frequent patients we found on our front porch, and those who needed transportation to hospitals, the timing of our trip to renew visas was most unfortunate.

Realizing the great need for someone to replace us while we were gone, we prayed earnestly, "Lord, whom will You send?"

That was when Gayle Haberkam informed Paul and me of her desire to take over for us, so we could go on furlough. Gayle, a friend from Montana, who had spent many years in emergency-room management, would be ideal for the job.

Therefore, about a month after the initial fighting and evacuation from Lay Klo Yaw, Gayle and her two sons, Bradley, age 16, and Micah, 14, arrived in Thailand, and we loaded them and their luggage into Old Trusty Rusty for the lengthy ride back to our home.

I found it hard to believe that just a few weeks before our friends' arrival, shells and mortars had echoed throughout the mountains with deafening noise. Now all appeared quiet. The rainy season still lingered, and gray skies hovered over us; but as Old Trusty Rusty descended the last mountain road toward our Thailand home, Gayle peered for the first time at the Moei River meandering below while Burma's steep, rugged mountains loomed beyond the other shore.

Gayle's eyes grew large with wonder, and the look on her face was priceless when she exclaimed, "I didn't realize you were this close to Burma!"

For at least half a week, she and her sons overcame jet lag. Then because I became ill again and had to rest for several days, Paul and our younger children took Gayle each morning to introduce her to villagers and to meet "her patients" among them, especially those who were scheduled for surgeries. Paul also took her and her boys up to the mountain retreat center to visit with our evacuated students, teachers, and other staff.

Our friend Gayle—who is now an inspiration to us all and an untiring servant for the Thai and Karen people—in those early days was undergoing the same process of adjustment (sometimes called, "culture shock") that most new missionaries face. She would return after hours out in the rain, going from hut to hut with Paul, and share with me later how she would slip and slide and fall in the mud; how someone had the audacity to spit betel nut juice on her shoes; or how a baby had urinated all over her.

In little time, though, Gayle adapted amazingly well to her new surroundings. As her small frame would scurry from place to place, she would climb up bamboo ladders, kneel beside the sick, and impart Jesus' love along with her medical expertise. Soon our porch was filled most every morning with patients, young and old, from both Thai and Burmese villages.

One day we experienced the kind of fright that only parents can feel. When Gayle, Anna, and Josiah were walking together toward our nearest village to visit the sick, suddenly fighting erupted with bullets flying and people scurrying to find shelter. (Later we discovered that Burmese soldiers had actually crossed the river into Thailand and entered the homes of Karen soldiers to shoot them!)

We breathed more easily when our children and Gayle returned safely. They had heard the shooting, but didn't actually see the people involved.

As soon as we had helped the schoolchildren escape across the border into Thailand, we became the object of frequent visits from Thai government and United Nations (U.N.) officials. What were mild intrusions into our lives turned into dreaded encounters for each of our Karen students, perhaps even more traumatizing than the evacuation itself. All their lives, the children had lived in fear of the Burmese army. Because of persecution in Karen State, the school had already changed locations five times when we first arrived on the Thailand side of the Moei.

Before their days at Lay Klo Yaw, many of those Karen youngsters had hidden in the jungle with their families, awaiting the army's retreat. After attacks and in the hope of returning home, they would find their villages burned down and the area planted with lethal landmines. Some of our students had witnessed horrible brutality to relatives and friends. And those memories made them even more attached to their school "family."

The love of Jesus was like a healing balm to them. Also, living inside the Thai border had brought some safety and security to our schoolchildren, but now their enemy wasn't the Burmese. It was well-meaning U.N. officials wanting the students to go to refugee camps. Moreover, Thai officials tried to encourage the children to return to Karen State, Burma. Soon, those young people—who normally welcomed every visitor with broad, sunny smiles—became introverted and fearful of strangers.

We could clearly see that the students in our temporary school at the mountain retreat center wanted to stay together. We tried our best to convince the government and U.N. officials to let us keep the children, but the officials were noncommittal. Therefore, we used our remaining days in Thailand to educate our medical worker Gayle in the reasons why our precious 120 students needed to stay together and in their school, however temporary it remained.

All too soon, the hour arrived for us to return to the United States to renew our visas. We left everything and everyone in the care of the school principal Blet Jaw, also Gayle Haberkam, Thara Eh K'Nyaw, and our daughter Emily. We trusted them to continue the work, together with the rest of the teachers and staff.

Gayle promised to mediate with officials if the need arose while we were gone. Meanwhile, she would keep busy with medical work among the villages and also during her morning "clinics" on our front porch. With Paul and me desperately needing a rest, God couldn't have chosen better replacements. Gayle was, indeed, His choice for that time, her sons Bradley and Micah laboring with her every step. Leaving Emily and "our people" wasn't easy, but we knew that our work was left in very capable hands.

At dawn, we loaded the few carry-on suitcases and our two sleepy children into Old Trusty Rusty. Gayle, Bradley, and Micah came along, too, taking advantage of better shopping for the school and themselves while in Mae Sot. (Gayle's older son Bradley was an excellent driver for the return trip because of his experience driving trucks and other heavy equipment on a Montana farm.) Paul would drive us to the bus station at Mae Sot, where the four of us would board a bus for the tiresome trip to Bangkok's airport area.

As we pulled away from our home, Anna began to cry, sobbing, "I don't want to leave Thailand. I love it here."

I told her we loved Thailand, too, but we had to return to America to renew our visas. It was the law. Anyway, we'd return to Thailand in a few months. "Time will fly!" I assured her. But nothing comforted our little girl, and her brother Josiah didn't look happy either. Over time, however, Anna's tears subsided, and we all reached the bus station in Mae Sot. Hugging each of the Haberkams, we thanked them profusely.

Our bus eventually reached Bangkok where a taxi transferred the four of us to a hotel for the night. Then early the next morning, Paul, Josiah, Anna, and I were soon soaring above a cushion of clouds, heading back to the United States, back to a totally different environment from the primitive land and people we had grown to love. As I closed weary eyes, my thoughts strayed to earlier times when the two older girls and I lived near Washington's wide Columbia River, then later in Montana with its glacial mountains and abundant wildlife. Oh, how things had changed . . .

CHAPTER 5

Vagabond Years

As our plane continued east, I pictured the scenic Columbia River Gorge again where, long ago, my family at that time lived temporarily in a used camper on our newly purchased mountain property. My husband worked nearby, building our "dream house" amid tall fir trees that gently danced with the west winds blowing through the Gorge.

All went well until those winds turned bitterly cold, and the drafty camper caused serious respiratory problems for our four-year-old daughter Maria. A doctor diagnosed her condition as "chronic pneumonia," and he advised that we find a warmer place to live.

Friends from my White Salmon church, Bethany and Alan Young, came to our rescue by inviting all four of us to share their family's roomy house, situated not too far from our property.

While my husband allowed our girls and me to move to the other residence during those cold months (so Maria could gain back her health), he chose to stay in the camper to spend as many of his free hours as possible for building on the house.

In the meantime, our eleven-year marriage was disintegrating. It was not a challenge for me to love my husband, because I truly loved him. The challenge was my living fully for God when, at the same time, staying united in love with a person who, more and more, demonstrated his negative attitude toward my faith. Then when our daughters sweetly sang *Jesus Loves Me* and other children's hymns, their father's annoyance grew.

While the apostle Paul's counsel in 2 Corinthians 6:14 pricked my conscience for choosing to marry an *unbeliever*, I now could understand that God had wanted to save me from many difficulties and heartaches. I held on by faith to His promise in 1 John 1:9, *If we confess our sins, He is faithful and righteous to forgive us our sins and to cleanse us from all unrighteousness.* Later, I would also take comfort in another of Paul's texts found in 1 Corinthians 7:15, *Yet if the unbelieving one leaves, let him leave; the brother or the sister is not under bondage in such cases, but God has called us to peace.* I must admit, however, that my heart felt as if it were ripping into shreds when I faced my husband's ultimatum: either I quit teaching the children about God and keeping the Sabbath, or he would start divorce proceedings.

I pleaded with him to accept my love as enough, pledging to do everything I could to make him happy—except to compromise my faith. But my husband's mind was made up, and there was no way I could convince him otherwise.

As I looked back on our years together, I could detect many instances when the Holy Spirit was nudging my husband, trying to woo him to our beloved Savior. But God also grants us the freedom to choose not to heed such "coaxing times."

The dark days of divorce did contain a few bright places. First, I was grateful to receive child support. Although a small amount, it would prove a blessing in the months to come. I also felt blessed when my husband granted me sole parental custody of our daughters. That custody would make it legally possible for Emily and Maria to accompany me when I visited family in Sweden.

Throughout the heartbreak of divorce and ensuing years, I learned that God could still give *beauty for ashes, the oil of joy for mourning*, and even the *garment of praise for the spirit of heaviness . . .* (from Isaiah 61:3, KJV).

And I honestly did praise God for giving the girls and me a comfortable place of refuge, a truly nurturing home for us—even before my husband's ultimatum. Alan and Bethany's warm hospitality proved to be a training ground for my daughters and me, training that would, years later, enhance our ministries.

Bethany was a nurse by profession, and their child Kayla had been born a beautiful, healthy baby. At eight months old, however, Kayla barely survived sudden infant death syndrome (SIDS), and was left with extensive brain damage. Their sweet child with cerebral palsy couldn't talk or walk, and was totally dependent upon family members.

During our time in this home, Kayla was a tall girl in her teens with all the traits of a baby. She would laugh, coo, and cry. I watched Bethany, along with others in the family, tenderly care for the girl, cheerfully feeding her, changing her, singing to her, and communicating such love.

Bethany was also a wonderful role model for my daughters. Even four-year-old Maria followed the other mother around, performing small tasks "to help Kayla." I will be eternally grateful, because my daughters and I learned much about Christian commitment from this family during those months.

There came a time, however, when the three of us needed to leave our friends' sheltering "nest." After a money gift arrived for airfare, I found reasonably priced tickets and made reservations to visit my family in Sweden. Moreover, I knew I had to learn to manage on my own now as a single parent.

While the girls and I prepared to travel to the land of my childhood, however, I suddenly realized my daughters had no presentable clothing for the trip. Emily and Maria had outgrown almost everything, and my family wouldn't understand their being dressed so poorly.

Lord, please . . .

Driving through the town of Stevenson, Washington, farther west downriver where we had once lived, I felt impressed to stop by a community service center to say hello (and goodbye) to my friends there.

As soon as my daughters and I entered the building, the women greeted us excitedly. "Come!" they urged. "We just received a shipment of girls' clothing."

To our amazement, there were only two sets of clothes, but one set was in Emily's exact size, and the other clothes were in Maria's smaller size! And they were quality outfits as if tailored just for my daughters—skirts, tights, turtlenecks, blouses, dresses, jackets, underwear, and even snowsuits—all surplus from a *Swedish* mail-order company. And Sweden was where we were headed the very next day! Much to my motherly relief, no one would be able to call my children "neglected." God, indeed, does care.

With gratitude still lingering in my heart, I returned to Sweden and my family for a while. Now without a husband, I didn't arrive empty-handed. I felt rich, because with me were my two precious daughters (with brand-new Swedish-made wardrobes).

Despite the child support we received monthly, I quickly discovered we needed more for everyday expenses. That's when God seemed to intervene by providing us with a place to live at a self-supporting missionary school in Sweden, where I would serve as a translator. Soon I found myself the sole cook in addition to working on translations in the evenings. Although I was grateful for the additional income, those responsibilities cut deeply into my quality time with Emily and Maria.

Returning to America, I worked as a housekeeper, because that job allowed me to keep my daughters with me. Then office duties were added to my already busy schedule. I again found myself struggling, because my calling as a mother (and now as a homeschool teacher) kept getting put on hold. I watched as eight-year-old Emily cared for her younger sister when I longed to be the one to nurture and teach my children. But I was able to offer Emily some "home-economic" instructions in household chores, which included preparing simple recipes during those days. Also, Emily and Maria were learning to read. And right next to my office was a small library where the girls occupied themselves by devouring mission stories. (These, I learned later, planted valuable seeds for our future service in a foreign field.)

Throughout the weeks that followed, we began to experience the plight of those who are poor, those who have to "toil for their daily bread"—and, sadly, those who are looked down upon.

"Pray, girls!" became our motto as we prayed ourselves through all difficulties. Praying, we went about our daily chores. Praying, we sang. Praying, we worshipped. And praying, we would drift off to sleep at night.

Eventually, God provided a new place for us in Washington State, this time way up a steep mountain in a small community of like believers. Although the road became dangerous in winter, my adventurous spirit welcomed the challenge of both the road and the little cottage we came to call home. The place had no running water, and the girls and I shared a large bed in the single room. This was one of the places my daughters gleaned some of their happiest childhood memories, because there in that cottage we spent our time *together*. Moreover, we were able to begin a more structured homeschooling program.

Ever since the divorce, I had desperately tried to be frugal and make ends meet by working in any way possible. I finally turned exclusively to housecleaning, because as the girls joined me, they acted as my assistants with smaller tasks, and also worked on their studies.

A friend, who was a woman of strong mind and character, kept challenging me to take everything to God, including our finances. With her wise counsel in mind, I found myself developing an even sweeter faith experience during those days.

The long walks together with my daughters in woods and meadows, our time reading and talking, even sledding and just having fun, proved quite healing. And all the while, God provided our needs—and more life lessons, soon to become invaluable.

In the midst of this healing, the same woman-friend urged, "Go to the South! It's cheaper to live there."

"But I don't have any money for such a trip," I protested.

Soon thereafter, some friends contacted me by phone. "We did your taxes!" they exclaimed.

"You did what?"

"Your taxes, and you have a large refund coming."

Even with that unexpected refund, we still needed more money for the trip. Also, I must truthfully admit not really wanting to leave that pleasant mountain community. But the next surprise came from the owner of our cottage, informing me they were selling the place. So we had no choice but to move. And that was exactly when an envelope was slipped into my hand, an envelope containing just what I needed to finance the rest of our trip to the Southeast.

Again and again, our needs were provided, and obstacles were removed. Was this because God knew my spiritual frailty and was teaching me to trust more in Him, a necessity for possible dark days ahead? Or was He simply preparing us for a greater work, a ministry to a poor and persecuted people?

As the girls and I traveled, little did we realize we would soon set a record in moving from place to place. Later we counted those places where we lived, however briefly, during our "vagabond years"—twenty-four different homes!

Friends had told me how beautiful Tennessee's Smoky Mountains were. So off we headed toward those mountains in our nation's Southeast. Singing, we rode along scenic routes, the girls having memorized most songs, both Scripture choruses and hymns.

Visiting with another friend along the way, I watched her circle a place on my *Road Atlas* map of Tennessee. "That's a special ministry you should visit on your way farther east," she said. But I had no intention of stopping at that place, because we were heading for the Smoky Mountains!

After a weary, long day of driving and not spotting one sign directing us to those elusive mountains, I realized we were hopelessly lost. So I pulled over at a service station with my map and asked about our location.

The attendant pointed to the circle my friend had drawn, and exclaimed, "You're right here!"

I looked at the girls and admitted, "We're so tired. Let's ask the people at this ministry if they'll allow us to use their restroom to wash up; then we'll sleep in the car."

Our weariness instantly fled when we were received like long, lost friends; moreover, those welcoming people convinced us that their home, not our car, was the place for us to rest—and not for just one night, but for several.

While visiting those hospitable folks, we learned of a vacant house in need of some "house-sitters." And, yes, the owners would be happy to have us there. Sight unseen, we accepted their offer. Again and again, we were learning to trust God and His people throughout our journey.

Although not situated in the Smoky Mountains, this place was in the hilly parts of Tennessee—with its lush green grasses and white rail fences. And the home was furnished with all the conveniences we had left behind years before. Best of all, it had shelves and shelves of inspiring books. Again, we spent many a late night, reading.

"Just one more chapter . . ." the girls would beg. Mostly they were stories of God's servants through the ages, faith stories, angel encounters, and missionary biographies. My daughters still treasure those memories of falling asleep after "just one more chapter," as had been our habit since their earliest years.

The same friend back in Washington State, who had urged me to trust God with our finances and to head to the Southeast, now phoned me about a "most godly man" who happened to live in the Southeast and who would make the "best father and husband." She was persistent in her conviction that we would be a "perfect match." So with some reluctance, I agreed to meet him.

Eddie was, indeed, a wonderful man of God. I came to admire him for his consistent faith and irrepressible joy in the Lord. In addition, at six-foot-one, he had a Southern Georgia drawl that sounded melodic to me. The brown curly hair atop his head matched his well-trimmed beard that didn't quite hide his dimples when he grinned (which was often). True sincerity, always present in his hazel eyes, was a welcome part of his character.

Moreover, I discovered that Eddie had played baseball since about eight years of age, and he continued playing with Little League until he joined a minor baseball league for a season. While attending a junior college, he again picked up a baseball and helped his team win the junior college championship; and that year, he was voted "Most Valuable Player."

Soon, though, with college and baseball behind him, Eddie joined his father's business, subcontracting to package-delivery companies. And more recently, Eddie spent time in Amish communities, where he had taught at a Christian school. He found joy in the simplest of things and seemed born with a "green thumb" as he delighted in gardening. He loved hard, physical work, and—best of all—he loved God. Because of that love, he wasn't afraid to witness about Jesus. Neither did he hesitate to help anyone in need.

After several months of courtship, Eddie and I were married in Tennessee—in the foothills of the beautiful Smoky Mountains!

2

The Oil of Joy for Mourning

CHAPTER 6

Grizzlies and Glaciers

Eddie moved in with the three of us at the Tennessee home God had provided when Emily, Maria, and I were weary pilgrims and became house-sitters. Soon, however, word came that the owners needed their house back.

God was apparently working behind the scenes again, this time arranging for us to move to Montana. In three months a cabin would be available for us near Glacier National Park, way out in the wilderness. Consequently, we needed a place to stay in the meantime.

While still in Tennessee, after church one weekend we were invited to have lunch with some friends at their house. Late that afternoon, the phone rang at our friends' home. It was another couple—strangers to us—who called, saying they were leaving the next morning and needed house-sitters while they were away for three months.

Three months? That was exactly how long we needed temporary housing before moving to Montana. We hadn't told anyone about our situation, but God knew, and He answered our prayers with a beautiful country home. We were grateful, also, for the generous and trusting Christians who owned that house and willingly handed over their keys to us.

Three months later the Montana wilderness welcomed our

family as we drove down a long lane to the cabin that would become our next home. To our surprise and delight, a grizzly bear crossed the road ahead of us (the first of fourteen grizzlies we would see while living there).

The property consisted of a large house on the shore of the North Fork River with Glacier National Park's snowcapped mountains towering beyond. Because the rent was way above our income, arrangements had been made for good friends with six daughters (and large dogs) to join us. Our family moved into the smaller guest cabin that was connected to a greenhouse, only a stone's throw away from the larger house.

Because of Eddie's good-natured personality and having taught church school, he was much more qualified than I to homeschool Emily and Maria. After all, English was his first language whereas Swedish was mine!

Besides scholarly subjects, Eddie taught our girls important skills they still practice today. Always with a smile, he showed them how to sweep carefully—even in the corners and behind the furniture where most people would never even look. He also taught them "faithfulness in the little things," like the art of folding laundry "just right," how to make a neat bed, and the secret to keeping the refrigerator sweet smelling and in order. I hadn't considered those skills particularly important for our own house every time we cleaned. But Eddie's labor of love bore fruit, and today we're grateful for his gentle instruction both in scholarly subjects and in practical domestic skills.

One of our grizzly-bear encounters occurred on a day Eddie was out in back of our cabin at the woodpile. Little Moriah, our neighbors' youngest daughter, enjoyed her time as "helper" to Eddie, whose sunny disposition attracted children like a human magnet—even in the midst of stacking wood. The rest of the girls, ours included, were playing nearby at the edge of a steep bank that led down to the river.

We felt lavishly blessed to have this as the children's playground.

Our Maria was seven years old at that time, a small girl with a sensitive nature. When she spotted the neighbors' barking dogs below, she noticed immediately that they had picked up speed as their paws clawed the dirt while climbing toward her and her playmates up on the riverbank.

Feeling uneasy, Maria quickly made her way back down to our cabin. Within minutes, the rest of the girls stormed through the doorway, crying—all except our Emily. She was motioning excitedly and with obvious joy as she exclaimed, "Mom, a grizzly with three cubs was chasing us!"

I peered out the front door and saw the bear, enormous and enthralling, but also terrifying, standing atop the bank in the very spot where the children had been playing. One moment the bear raised up on her hind legs, and the next moment she was right near our front door, lumbering alongside the cabin toward the woodpile where Eddie and little Moriah were busy.

When my husband heard the panic in my voice, he didn't hesitate. Scooping up Moriah, he shot through the back doorway and in one fell swoop, turned the door's sturdy deadbolt. Then everyone huddled safely inside until "Mama Bear" led her cubs elsewhere.

Many a time we encountered those majestic animals during the months we lived on the fringes of Glacier National Park. Grateful for the neighbors' dogs that dutifully warned us with raucous barking, we also appreciated them and their keen sense of smell for wild creatures of any kind.

Although our family enjoyed living in this wilderness that seemed fresh every morning with new wonders from nature in a kaleidoscope of colors, I knew we couldn't continue living there. We were expecting a baby and, therefore, had to find a larger home.

Please, Lord, we need a place to live with lower rent and more room.

Every one of us was joyful about the baby, but there simply

wasn't enough space anymore for another person in our cabin—not even for a tiny person!

Every time I prayed, an idea kept popping into my mind, an impression that grew stronger and stronger. I recalled that a friend had told another friend about a house they were interested in renting; it was located in a Northern Washington national forest.

But, Lord, that was a long time ago.

Dismissing the idea, I still found that house intruding in my prayers. But I kept ignoring those promptings as ridiculous. After all, it was highly unlikely the place would be available now, many years later.

God also knew the future, which He mercifully concealed from Eddie and me. In His goodness, He was ready to provide us with the larger place we needed and where we would have more friends for support later on.

I finally decided to mention to Eddie about my long-ago memory of a house in Washington State. And his reply was totally unexpected.

"Go now," he urged, "and call! I'll stay with the children."

Driving down the snowy road with my address book lying beside me, I marveled at the North Fork River glistening in the sunshine. I was already feeling nostalgic about leaving this peaceful place and knew we would all miss it. Soon the Pole Bridge Mercantile came into view, a quaint, old-fashioned building from years past. I carefully made my way to the weathered pay phone clinging to the outside wall. With stiff, cold fingers, I mustered the courage to make the call.

"Yes, the house is empty, but it's spoken for," came the voice over the line. Within a day, however, the renters cancelled. And now the place was ours. The monthly cost was half our existing rent, and the house even had three bedrooms. God again provided, this time for our growing family. (And I was growing, too, as I neared our baby's due date.)

We quickly packed up our few belongings, hugged our neighbors goodbye, squeezed into our car, then headed toward Washington State's Colville National Forest. As we neared the area where we soon would live, the sight made my heart leap. Called Aspen Valley, it reminded me of Sweden, the aspens looking much like the birch trees common in my former Scandinavian country.

Although it was the dead of winter, not long after our arrival we found a welcoming local church. For months, Emily and Maria had been earnestly studying their Bibles in preparation for baptism. And despite February's freezing temperatures, our daughters decided to dedicate their lives to God publicly in baptism during an evening service before our new congregation.

Afterward, Eddie surprised Emily and Maria with a gift for each of them, a pretty handkerchief with embroidered pastel flowers.

Later, we drove happily home from church through glittering snow. Lighting our kerosene lanterns and preparing for bed, we had no idea that in just a few hours, another daughter would enter our family.

"Eddie, we need to get to the hospital—now!"

As my husband slowly awoke, I noticed something was not quite the same about him. But I couldn't define what it was, not yet.

Driving down the moonlit road with two sleepy girls in back, I kept quietly asking God to keep me from giving birth in the car. And we did make it to the hospital—in time. A healthy girl, Anna Grace with the cutest little face, was born that Valentine's night. Barely tipping the scale at just above six pounds, Baby Anna was much smaller at birth than her older sisters had been; each of them had weighed in at 8 pounds.

A few days later, after we were all settled at home with our sweet baby, I decided to broach a sensitive subject. "Something's wrong, Eddie. You seem different."

"Yes," he admitted. "I know."

This otherwise very patient man had suddenly begun to lose his temper at times. And this normally social person was becoming withdrawn. Also a strange trickle of saliva on one side of his mouth offered another clue.

We decided to see the same doctor who had just delivered Anna. And as soon as the physician saw Eddie and heard our concerns, she immediately started evaluating his reflexes, balance, and more. That very day she ordered an MRI, and we later met with a young surgeon who peered at us through bloodshot eyes. I couldn't help noticing his trembling fingers as he jotted down notes.

The doctor's words hit like a blow to my solar plexus: "I'm sorry, Eddie, but you have a tumor in the frontal lobe of your brain, and you need immediate surgery; but it's high-risk. There's a 50-percent chance you won't survive the operation."

When the surgeon walked out, allowing us time to evaluate the news privately, Eddie exclaimed, "I won't have that doctor cutting on me. Did you see the way his hands shook?"

After some discussion with each other and with the Lord, we decided that if the surgeon were willing to pray with us, we would go ahead and have him perform the surgery.

When the doctor returned to the room, I looked intently into those tired eyes and asked, "Are you comfortable praying with us before you operate?" His affirmative answer calmed our fears. Then upon surrendering any leftover worries to our Master Physician, Eddie and I felt some peace.

Not too long after Baby Anna's birth, Eddie was pushed on a gurney through the corridors of a Spokane hospital. His arms encircled tiny Anna as she lay atop his chest—until they reached a set of double doors. As soon as I kissed Eddie's forehead and lifted the baby, my husband was whisked away. Then Emily, Maria, Anna, and I waited six long hours.

Finally, the surgeon came out and met with us, saying he had successfully removed a tumor the size of a grapefruit from Eddie's frontal lobe. My husband was in Recovery and was doing well. But I felt numb.

How could something that large be inside Eddie's head?

After each bend in the road of our lives together, there seemed to lurk another new challenge. This time it was the surgeon's prediction: "Eddie's cancer is a glioblastoma, stage four, highly aggressive, and he has only about a year left to live. We won't be able to operate again, so next time the tumor grows that large, there'll be nothing we can do except to help with the pain."

Only one year left to live . . .

Through the months that followed, we witnessed the constant care of our heavenly Father. Eddie wasn't well enough to work, and with us living way out in a wilderness, our survival itself was a miracle indeed. We never voluntarily shared our plight with others, not a word. Yet God provided our many needs in miraculous ways.

Life went on and, although we took precautions, I learned I was pregnant again. All of us rejoiced—especially Eddie when learning the baby was a boy. My husband exclaimed, "I can teach him everything I know!"

But I wondered, *Will Eddie even live long enough to see his son?*

CHAPTER 7

A Mosquito in a Jar

It was early morning, and my friend Eileen had slept restlessly during the night. She kept hearing something, which she later described as sounding like a mosquito in a jar.

Eileen rose early that morning at the prompting of her three-year-old son David, asking her to go outside and join him in picking wild strawberries. So, together with their buckets, they soon roamed behind their cabin, which was situated about 400 feet from our cabin in the Colville National Forest.

While hunting for the delicious wild edibles, little David said, "Mom, I hear someone calling 'Help me!'"

Eileen strained to listen, but heard nothing. Once in a while, her son would tug on her arm and exclaim, "Mommy, someone *is* calling for help!"

Although my friend was unable to hear anything unusual that crisp morning, David wouldn't let go of his distress. So Eileen decided to use their Walkie-talkie to call her husband. Soon thereafter, the threesome hiked down to our cabin, sharing how little David insisted someone was pleading for help.

Eileen added, "I had a restless night, because I kept hearing something like the sound of a mosquito trapped in a jar."

Together our families decided to form two search parties—just in case. We quickly gathered some blankets and other items we thought helpful in the event we should find someone in need of assistance.

Off we drove in separate cars. It seemed logical to start east of our cabins on a Forest Service road that led to a couple of small lakes. Eddie, our older girls, Baby Anna, and I rode slowly along with our car windows down, listening carefully and searching the passing woods for a sign of anything out of the ordinary.

Glancing over at Eddie, I smiled. He had healed well from the brain surgery and was more like himself again—for now.

About a mile from our cabin, I suddenly spotted an overturned Jeep way down an embankment. "Eddie!" I exclaimed. "There's a car down there!"

We quickly notified our neighbors over our Walkie-talkies, telling them about the overturned vehicle. While the children and I waited on the road, the men ventured down the bank. Drawing closer to the Jeep, they heard, "Help me!"

It was Hollis, another remote neighbor. Apparently, he had flown out of the Jeep when it veered off the road, and the poor man had been lying there helpless since six o'clock the previous evening. (Later we learned that his pelvis and other bones were fractured.) While lying there, Hollis had found a nearby branch and reached with it into the Jeep onto its steering wheel. Throughout the night as he gathered enough strength in spurts, he would honk the horn with that branch. He hoped the noise would ward off wild animals and, at the same time, gain our attention. In such a deserted place, Hollis knew we were his only hope for survival.

Eileen then realized the beeping horn was what kept disturbing her sleep, and that faraway noise was what sounded to her like a mosquito in a jar. Amazingly, little David kept hearing Hollis' cries for help when nobody else could!

Eddie now remained with Hollis where he lay near the Jeep. The rest of us went in search of a way to call an ambulance. None of our three cabins had phone service in such a wilderness. But we did have a key to the house of our landlord who was gone at that time—and he owned a satellite phone! So we ladies were able to call for help and give directions.

Meanwhile, Eddie talked with Hollis and prayed for him. At the same time, my husband was trying to ward off various insects that seemed intent on making the injured man even more miserable. Later, watching my husband do his best to keep Hollis comfortable (using the blankets and pillows we'd brought along), I remembered that ever since we first met Hollis and his wife, Eddie had been praying for the man. My husband hoped Hollis would come to know Jesus as his Savior and learn other Bible truths.

Hours passed before the rescue team could figure out how to get the ambulance near enough below the accident scene to bring their patient safely down the steep hill for transport to a medical center. Then later we learned that after Hollis was evaluated at the Colville hospital, their patient was airlifted to Seattle for surgery on his crushed pelvis and for specialized care for his other injuries. Meanwhile, emergency personnel were finally able to contact Hollis' wife, who had been gone for a few days; she could then travel on to Seattle and encourage her husband.

How we rejoiced to have been able to partake in the rescue effort—and marveled at how God had used a small boy to convince his mom and others to form a search party!

During the following weeks, at first we heard that Hollis might be paralyzed for life. But as our church family joined us in prayer for our neighbor, the updates became more optimistic. And soon to everyone's gratitude, Hollis kept improving until he was even able to walk again.

When our neighbor returned home during his convalescence, he asked Eddie to study the Bible with him. And after weeks of those studies, Hollis gave his life to God and was baptized. He recovered so well that he was even able to return to his job at a hardware store.

CHAPTER 8

Envelopes and Matthew 6:8

Because Eddie's surgeon had given him only a year to live, my husband couldn't apply for any kind of employment without revealing the truth about the virulent cancer growing again in his brain. Therefore, with Eddie's shortened life expectancy, we were advised at the hospital to apply for disability compensation. He had worked his entire adult life and had faithfully paid into Social Security; so we filled out the government forms and submitted them. During that long waiting time, my hospital bills and those of Eddie's surgery were stacking up, and we were totally dependent upon God for *His* "disability compensation."

Once in a while, I'd exclaim, "Eddie, we have no food!"

"Don't worry about it," he would reply. "God will provide." This was my husband's standard answer whenever the cupboard looked bare, always with his slow Southern drawl and a broad grin.

Sometimes I became agitated and would tell him, "That's easy for you to say. You don't have to cook!"

Always, though, God chose to care for us in various ways, like with envelopes mailed to us with money inside from people wishing to remain anonymous. Because we were uncomfortable about sharing our needs with others, those financial gifts seemed outright miraculous.

One weekend, Eddie wasn't feeling well and stayed home while the rest of our family headed to church where we usually attended. Suddenly, I changed my mind and called out to the children, "Let's go to the Colville church today!"

Upon entering the foyer, I accompanied the older girls to their Sabbath school class. Then I carried Anna through the hallway and headed toward the sanctuary. A man, whom I'd never seen before, came up to me and quietly slipped an envelope into my hands with the words, "God told me to give this to you." Later, I found the envelope contained $40, just what we needed for groceries that next week! (To this day, I don't know who that man was.)

While driving home that afternoon, I marveled at God's care for us. At the same time, I had one more request, just thinking the prayer: "Lord, we need $20 more in order to be able to fuel our car for the week."

Checking our mailbox, I found a letter from someone on the East Coast who had felt impressed to send the exact cost of fuel I had secretly requested—just as Matthew 6:8 promises, . . . *for your Father knows what you need before you ask Him.*

I have to confess, however, that my faith wavered whenever I realized we were running out of supplies and food again. Soon there would be nothing left on our shelves, and then that dreaded morning arrived after we finished the last of our food at breakfast.

Snow was falling heavily upon what had already accumulated around our house. But we all bundled up for our daily walk anyway. Even little Anna was placed in a snowsuit bag (made for babies) and was securely tied onto the sled. Those walks in the fresh air were a practice all five of us enjoyed.

After hiking up our drive, we high-stepped through a snowy berm to the gravel road that had previously been plowed, but now held more fresh, fluffy snow, easy to walk through, even with our sled. And with each step, I silently prayed, "Father God, we need food plus shampoo, toothpaste, laundry soap, and other supplies."

"Eddie!" I called. "Do you hear a truck coming our way?"

To our surprise, a truck turned right into our drive and drove straight to our house and parked. So we all turned around and trudged back.

Eventually, I recognized the driver. "Becky, what in the world are you doing here in this weather?"

Becky was a friend who had recently moved to our area and was newly married. We soon learned that she had set aside that day for sewing and baking bread. Her husband, on the other hand, insisted she change her plans.

"Honey, we're going to the grocery store!" he exclaimed.

"Why?" she asked. "We don't need anything."

"God told me to buy food and other stuff for Eddie's family," he said.

At the store Becky would select a normal size of an item, but her husband would insist they get the *family* size instead. He also handed her "goodies" to place in the loaded cart.

That day God moved mightily through those generous friends to provide for our family. Tears filled my eyes when I spotted all the bags stacked inside their truck. Later in the house, I noticed that every item we needed was inside those bags: toothpaste, laundry detergent, hand soap, honey, vegetables, fruit—and even "goodies"!

Many similar such scenarios occurred during Eddie's illness, especially before his disability compensation arrived. For example, one time we were sitting in our car, waiting for sunset. We had been out in nature after church, enjoying an unusually mild day. Now with Sabbath about to draw to a close, we knew there wasn't enough gas in the tank to make the journey home. I remember sitting there, gazing at the few pennies in my purse.

Father in Heaven, please, what shall we do? And as always, God already had the answer.

As soon as Sabbath ended at sundown, Eddie casually mentioned an envelope someone had handed him during church.

"Why didn't you open it?" I asked.

"Because it was Sabbath," he said, "and I thought it might have money inside. It's kind of thick."

Tucked into that envelope was $500 in cash! I cried. We felt incredibly rich, because we knew that immense gift would last us a long time. Filling our car's tank with gasoline that evening, we went on our way, praising our mighty God and thanking Him for the generous soul who, apparently, had carried out the Lord's will.

Another example of God's benevolence was when I had wished for some soy milk powder for our children. We lived without electricity and without other conveniences, not even a generator at that time, which would have made food preparation easier (with gadgets, such as an electric blender).

One day we received word about a parcel left with neighbors 14 miles down our snowy road—"a late Christmas present," I guessed.

When helping us with the cumbersome package, the neighbor cheerfully announced, "It looks like someone sent you fifty pounds of almonds!"

Backing up the car to his porch, I silently complained to God, *Almonds! Why didn't You send us soy milk powder instead? Nuts would be fine, Lord, if I could use my blender. And Anna can't eat nuts yet . . .*

With a sigh, I decided to share some of the nuts with our neighbor. When he opened the huge box, he hollered, "Not almonds—but soy milk powder!" And, again, there was no return address. It was from another anonymous giver. I suddenly felt ashamed, humbled—and very grateful.

After Eddie's disability compensation began to arrive monthly in our bank account, we heard that our rented house there in Northern Washington was being put up for sale. Eddie had been missing the South with its warmer weather and better gardening opportunities, so back to the Southeast we headed. But I wondered, was it God's will? Obstacles kept cropping up, also sickness and other unplanned "events" during our journey.

With Eddie seeming unusually healthy when we passed through Montana, the girls and I asked him if we could find a place there to live. But he sang out, "To the good old South we go!" So the five of us persevered just as Emily, Maria, and I had done about two years before in our search for the elusive Smoky Mountains.

When we passed through the Midwest, I found myself close to tears, because what was expected to be so simple—finding a home—had ended up becoming a major trial. Staying in motels became tedious and costly. In addition, houses were more expensive than we had been told.

One evening in Virginia, while we searched for a reasonably priced motel, I silently asked, "Lord, I wonder if this is how pregnant Mary felt while she and Joseph were looking for lodging in Bethlehem?"

That night God gave us a place with a weekly rate. To my delight, a Bible on the desk lay open to a promise I felt was just for us: *'For I know the plans that I have for you,' declares the Lord, 'plans for welfare and not for calamity to give you a future and a hope'* (Jeremiah 29:11). Moreover, the room was much like a suite, large enough that we would all be comfortable—and we could safely use the electric crockpot we had brought along.

When we attended church that Sabbath, a young couple befriended us, such kind, earnest people! Our friendship with them grew over the next few weeks.

As we looked at more houses, this time along curvy West Virginia roads, Eddie became quite ill. Back at the motel in Virginia, he was bedridden with a migraine and began vomiting. Meanwhile, my mind was in a whirl: *Is this the tumor returning as the surgeon had predicted?*

Our new friends from church called us one morning, sharing that they wanted to give us a gift of money, a very generous gift "to help with Eddie's health needs." I was reluctant to accept such a huge amount, but they were adamant, because God had impressed each of them with the same amount (unbeknown to the other) during their separate prayer times. And then Eddie, who was feeling better by then, told me that their gift was the exact amount that he had given his niece years before when she was somewhat destitute. Because of my husband's pre-existing condition, he didn't qualify for insurance—just for the monthly disability compensation that we "stretched" as best we could—so the monetary gift was, indeed, a blessing.

Next, some friends invited us to visit them in an Amish area where property prices were more affordable. In Amish country, we made even more friends who treated us like family. But we still couldn't find a suitable house we could afford.

Then people in Kentucky invited us to search for a home in their vicinity. While staying with them, when Eddie again became ill, I pleaded with God for a place where I could treat Eddie with "natural remedies." I reminded the Lord about our need for a juicer and for a bathtub for "fever treatments."

About that time our Kentucky friends received a phone call from a woman who was weeping. "I've asked God to send someone my way to stay at my guesthouse, and I told Him, if He didn't send any paying customers, would He, please, send someone with a great need? I will let your friends stay for free," she said. She had heard about our search for a home and urged us to come quickly, because her guesthouse was on the brink of foreclosure.

Soon we had that beautiful guesthouse all to ourselves: the kitchen with a professional juicer and a suite with a whirlpool-type tub, everything and more that I'd prayed for—and just in time!

While there, Eddie became totally bedridden, but it was a good place to care for him and a wonderful home for Emily, Maria, and little Anna for several weeks. Soon I realized that only one month remained before our baby's due date.

When I had previously asked Eddie if we could return to Montana, he was always firmly against it. And now, with a baby coming and Eddie so ill, I felt moved to call the friends who lived in the big house next to the cabin on the edge of Glacier National Park.

We hadn't been in contact for a long time, and the news they shared rang happily in my ears, "We are in the process of moving!"

I asked Eddie again about the large Montana house, and this time he relented, "Well, the Lord isn't providing anything else here; so we might as well go there."

Although the owner agreed to our renting the house as soon as we returned to Montana, I felt distressed. How would I lift my sick husband up out of bed and get him into the SUV? He couldn't even walk to the bathroom on his own. And I was so pregnant that I was unable to fit safely behind the steering wheel.

But I could still kneel as I prayed, "Lord, if it's Your will for us to go back to Montana, please help Eddie to be able to drive."

To my joy-filled wonder, the next morning Eddie sprang out of bed, singing and as jovial as ever while packing the car with all our belongings. (He had a knack for packing and did an excellent job.)

My husband was able to drive for five days straight, resting only at night. When we arrived at the wilderness home, he unpacked everything, put items in order, then crashed.

CHAPTER 9

Death Sentence

Nearing our baby's arrival time, all of us journeyed to stay with our friends who formerly had lived in the home we now inhabited. Their new residence was near the hospital in White Fish, Montana. While there, Eddie had started vomiting again because of intense headaches. We took him to the ER that day, and an MRI revealed a tumor the size of a grapefruit again.

Back at our friends' home, I answered the phone and heard, "Your husband has only six-to-seven weeks left to live."

Later when I walked quietly into the room where Eddie sat in a chair, I wondered how I would tell him. I felt like it was *me* who had just been given a death sentence.

"Eddie," I ventured, "the doctor called and said you have no more than six or seven weeks left to live, and there's nothing that can be done this time."

Were my eyes tricking me, or was my husband really smiling? Ever cheerful and full of faith, Eddie hearing of his impending death in no way changed his consistent Christian behavior.

Our friends' teenage daughters came to me, quite upset. "How can your husband just sit there and smile?"

I tried to explain to them how much Eddie loved Jesus and

how much he welcomed the thought of meeting his Savior "in a twinkling of an eye" on Resurrection Morning.

Josiah Jonathan was born that same night, weighing 11 pounds, 6 ounces! And Eddie did get to hold his son the next day. Because both Josiah and Jonathan were exemplary Bible characters, Eddie and I had spent some time discussing which name should come first if our child should be a boy, as predicted. When we read in 2 Kings 23:25 that Josiah *turned to the Lord with all his heart and with all his soul and with all his might,* the decision was made!

As I watched my husband cuddle our newborn, I hoped with every ounce of my being that little Josiah would grow up to have the same kind of relentless faith and compassion as his father.

All too soon some friends arrived from the Pacific Northwest to whisk Eddie away to an experimental therapy in Portland, Oregon. (We just couldn't let Eddie go without giving him one last chance at healing.)

The treatment failed. And when I also heard that Eddie had been moved to an intensive care unit at a Portland hospital, I quickly packed our car with all the extras needed for a newborn and toddler. With haste, I tucked Josiah into a car seat. Anna was also strapped into hers. Then Emily and Maria watched over the little ones for the long drive west.

Because of Eddie's critical condition, several members of his "Southern kin" flew to Portland to visit him at the hospital. What a blessing for my husband to have family at his bedside while the rest of us were traveling and couldn't arrive for several days!

The next few weeks we spent driving between that hospital and Alan and Bethany's mountain home above the Columbia River near White Salmon, Washington.

With the medical staff's permission, we were allowed to give Eddie carrot juice and wheatgrass juice through his feeding tube instead of the formulas usually administered. My husband remained in the ICU for twelve days, and then he began to improve.

Insisting upon leaving the hospital, he (and I) had to sign a waiver, because his doctor said Eddie was dying from the massive brain tumor.

Off we went, this time to stay at a home-health sanitarium; while there, Eddie received juices and raw foods as well as a few treatments in a hyperbaric chamber.

After spending three weeks at the sanitarium, we packed up our SUV, and we all headed back to Montana. Without warning in the middle of the night, our car broke down just as we entered Kalispell. Out of desperation, I called some friends I hoped could help us. They told us to call someone else from their church and gave us the number.

Mustering the courage to phone strangers at that horrible hour, I told them of our plight.

"Sure! We'll come and pick you up!" Those Good Samaritans came to our rescue that night, taking all six of us to their home.

Looking out the window of their guest cabin the next morning, I turned to Eddie and exclaimed, "This is the most beautiful place I've ever seen!" Then I described to him the larger, main log house, a pond, a creek, an orchard, and garden—all immaculately cared for. And most delightful was a golden retriever sleeping next to a deer by the pond! This was, indeed, a seeming paradise.

If I could have peered into the future, I would have been astonished to discover this "paradise" would eventually become our home. But first, God would perform another miracle . . .

Soon we were back up in our mountain wilderness near Glacier National Park, ready to tackle my husband's sickness with fresh vigor. We had declared all-out war on our enemy, cancer. And with the help of generator power, I kept busy making carrot juice, steeping herbal teas to store in amber bottles, and preparing other "brain formula herbs" according to my research. Eddie also consumed green barley powder and lots of raw fruits, vegetables, almonds, and flax seed. All of his diet was raw—except for steamed potatoes and cooked millet to give him a feeling of fullness and the warmth he needed during winter's chill.

Within three months, because Eddie's condition had remarkably improved, his doctor ordered another MRI and other tests. Upon reading the results, the neurosurgeon breezed into his office where my husband and I waited. The doctor shook his head in wonderment, exclaiming, "I've never seen anything like this in my life!" Then he pointed to the ceiling and said, "It must be the Man upstairs."

He told us that Eddie's tumor had shrunk to the size of a peanut! Only someone with a trained eye, however, could actually see the tiny spot on the MRI. He then described Eddie's brain as "beautiful." This was the same surgeon who, three months before, had given my husband six or seven weeks to live. The doctor now compared the previous ugly "films" of Eddie's brain—deformed by the hideous-looking tumor—with the recent pictures. What a difference! The surgeon's last words to us were, "Keep up whatever you're doing!"

We again began looking for a more dependable place of our own. But each time our search seemed promising, the door would shut. Juicing and preparing raw foods—plus a few cooked vegan dishes—way out in a wilderness were a huge challenge, especially with generator problems. Again and again, the generator would break down. Now we were running out of firewood, the propane tank was getting low, and because of new medical bills, we didn't have enough money to replace the fuel if it did run out. All we could do was pray for another place to live.

Meanwhile, we accepted an invitation for a meal together with several families. One of those families, who happened to be the Good Samaritans who rescued us during our middle-of-the-night car breakdown, presented us with a lot of clothes, nice hand-me-downs that would fit little Anna.

The next time I drove to town for groceries, I phoned to thank the kind woman for Anna's "new" clothes. I also invited her and her family to join us during the upcoming weekend for a meal at our house. That's when I heard they were leaving the following day for six months. They had been looking for a caretaker and had thought of asking us, but were told that we were happy where we were.

Swallowing my reluctance to share our situation with others, I revealed the truth to the woman, and that night we received the keys to the "dream log house with the golden retriever and deer resting together by a pond." This became our new home and was also "off the grid," but with alternative power that worked! And what a joy it was for all six of us to be able to live at such a beautiful, serene place . . .

Our family has always enjoyed music, and when we could afford lessons, Emily and Maria learned to play the piano and a few other instruments. Now that we lived in a larger home, I thought it would be a great time to get a piano, so the girls could renew their talents. I had saved $100 for it.

When we prayed about the piano, I recalled that there was an old one in our previous rental house in Aspen Valley. So I called our former landlord's satellite phone and inquired about the old piano. She told me that, actually, an auction company was there, and the next item in line was the piano!

"But you can have it for $100," she said, "if you come and get it."

A string of providential events followed and proved to me that God cared about our daughters and their musical need. First, we borrowed a trailer to haul from Montana to Washington State to claim the instrument. Next, our pastor loaned us his pickup truck for the trip. After we paid for and brought the piano home, it sat in the trailer, covered with a tarp for several days in our yard. Because Eddie was too ill to do anything about it, I prayed for God to find us help in moving it. After all, it wasn't good for the piano to sit out there in the elements, and we needed to return the trailer.

Then one day as I ventured out to get groceries, a woman whom I'd met at a funeral, was walking along the road. I rolled down my window and greeted her. Unexpectedly, something popped into my mind: *Tell her about the piano!* So I told her about my dilemma. She surprised me by saying her son-in-law had just arrived for a visit— and he was a professional piano mover! That same day, the young man came and moved the piano into our house—at no charge, an added blessing.

What was not a blessing were the mice that had built nests inside the instrument. We immediately evicted them, so the piano would be ready for the tuner the next day.

When the man arrived, he inspected the piano, then delivered bad news. "It's no use to try to tune this instrument," he said, "because it's too far out of tune and so old, the strings will break. And if your girls play such an out-of-tune piano, it might harm their sense of pitch."

But, Lord, wasn't this gift from You?

I told the piano tuner, "This was a gift from God. Please, go ahead and tune it while I go into the other room and pray."

A hint of a frown flashed across his face, but he agreed to try. During the next hour as I knelt in prayer by the bathtub, I kept hearing the tuner exclaiming over and over, "Amazing! Amazing!"

Apparently, the strings did not break. From then on, the piano sounded wonderful whenever our Emily or Maria would sit down and fill our house with the sounds of familiar hymns.

CHAPTER 10

Learning to Trust

It was evening and quite dark outside when we heard the helicopter hovering overhead. Although we had kept our SUV lights on and the horn honking, the helicopter and ambulance apparently still had a difficult time finding our wilderness abode.

I had never witnessed a grand-mall seizure before. So when Eddie experienced one, then lay lifeless on the bed, I immediately phoned 911. And by the time the helicopter landed, Eddie was conscious and even walking around as if nothing had happened. How embarrassed I felt when the paramedic and other emergency personnel rushed into our house!

Despite Eddie's normal behavior, however, the medics insisted my husband be transported to the hospital for evaluation. I dreaded what the MRI would show. In a few short hours, my worst fears were realized: the brain tumor that had shrunk to the size of a peanut about three months previously had returned with a vengeance. Now it was grapefruit-size again, lodged in the same frontal lobe.

It was as if Eddie's cancer had grown smart and found a way around the natural remedies that had helped prolong his time with us. Or perhaps Eddie's optimism had influenced him to give up his strict diet as soon as he had discovered how much the tumor had shrunk. (He had also begun eating cooked—instead of raw—vegan foods and occasional treats.)

One thing I do know is that Eddie's faith remained undaunted even with such a grim discovery. My husband continued to place God first in everything he did.

"I'm giving it all to Jesus," he said soon after his re-diagnosis.

"You're doing what?"

"I've had another birthday, and for this I'm grateful!" he announced.

For Eddie's birthday, his brother had sent him $60. That was a lot for us, because besides rent, groceries, old—and now, new—medical bills, there were the extra expenses that go hand-in-hand with two little ones in diapers.

After tithing, then purchasing groceries, I ventured, "Eddie, I'd like to spend the remaining $40 on diapers for Anna and Josiah . . ."

My husband was insistent. "Oh, no! I'm giving all the rest to the Lord."

I felt frustrated because the washing machine in our beautiful log house had broken down. The situation made me wonder, how did pioneer women ever accomplish anything besides washing cloth diapers for more than one child? On the other hand, I realized that Eddie's poor brain was literally being squeezed unmercifully. I also knew that the frontal lobe was the place where judgment, ethics, and other moral issues are normally "filtered" for right or wrong. And with Eddie's faith remaining intact despite his brain under such siege was, indeed, a miracle.

My husband was sleeping comfortably one early evening, and I knew I needed some "spiritual food" in order to deal with my frustration regarding his decision about the $40. So I took our children to an evangelistic seminar at our church.

After the meeting ended, I turned to a local doctor, a "brother in Christ," and asked, "Wasn't that a good sermon?"

"I couldn't hear a word of it," the doctor confessed. "All I could hear was God telling me to give you the money I have in my wallet. I'm sorry, Lena, but all I have is $40."

I thanked him politely, but felt my neck and face grow warm with embarrassment—not because of our neediness, but because of my lack of faith! When would I ever learn to trust God and His abundant care for Eddie, the children, and me? When would I actually relax and hold firmly onto God's hand, no matter the trials that lay ahead of us? Moreover, I hadn't told anyone about my discussion with Eddie regarding the $40 he wanted to give to the Lord. And despite my husband's horrendous condition, his faith never wavered, but mine did. How humbled and sad I felt!

With his condition rapidly declining, Eddie became bedridden and was unable to feed himself anymore. His swollen brain would turn this once-thoughtful husband and father into an unruly confused "child" who wanted to do things on his own, thus ending up as a heap on the floor.

"Girls," I would call, "come and help me! Daddy's on the floor again, and he's too heavy."

We all hurt to see him like this. And it took all of us "women"— Emily and Maria, now ages 13 and 10, even little Anna with her tiny arms adding to our efforts, helping to lift their "Daddy" off the floor and back onto the bed.

About this time, Hospice became involved. Those compassionate people brought a hospital bed with protective rails and other equipment to make our jobs easier. I was immensely grateful for their help.

It was easier now for me to keep Eddie clean and to coax food and water into his mouth and to prevent him from choking. But as his condition demanded more and more of my time, I found myself sinking into a deep state of fatigue, and I felt incredibly overwhelmed.

Lord, I can't handle this. What about Anna and little Josiah? I have no time for them. Emily and Maria have to do it all.

In that moment I realized I felt resentful, an attitude from which

I couldn't escape. Exasperated, I asked my daughters, "Would you mind if I drive the garbage to the dump? I need to pray."

Our 4-wheel-drive SUV had, indeed, become my prayer chamber, my only reprieve whenever I'd go after supplies or visit the dump as I did that day.

After emptying our large trashcan, I pulled off to the side and opened my heart to my heavenly Father. "Lord, I'm having an awful time with my attitude. I can't stand myself. I can't get rid of this resentment. Please, help me!"

There in that vehicle, a picture flashed into my mind, an image of Jesus in Eddie's place, lying on the bed. Then I heard God's gentle voice whisper, "The way you treat Eddie is the way you are treating Me."

You, Lord?

Although I hadn't deliberately mistreated Eddie, my attitude was one of resentment with a lack of compassion, and the comparison hit me hard. I broke down, sobbing and sobbing, asking for forgiveness. In those moments I could actually feel the heavy oppression of resentment lift and flee far, far away. Dabbing at my wet face with a tissue, I thanked God for this extraordinary victory. That day I was able to return home to care again for my husband, but now in a most tender, loving manner.

A few hours after midnight on New Year's Day, 2002, although Eddie had obviously sunk into a deep coma, he still struggled for breath. I stood at his bedside, holding his hand while our children slept soundly in their rooms. I'd been warned about the "death rattle," but nothing could have prepared me for those dreadful final moments. Numb with heartache, I sat down and quietly sang, *It is Well with my Soul,* and watched through the window for any hint of sunrise.

Later, the children and I huddled together on the sofa that cold January morning, waiting for someone from the funeral home to come and take our precious "Daddy" away.

Despite the bitter cold, Eddie's funeral commenced that very afternoon with a simple graveside service. Members of our church gathered around the five of us as we listened to the eulogy, soothing Bible promises, and the pastor's own words of encouragement.

Then, upon driving to a gas station on our way home, I felt utterly lost. I was struggling with thoughts of facing our empty house where Eddie had breathed his last that very morning.

As I fueled up our car, friends came along. "Lena, please, let us go home with you!" I smiled, gladly welcoming their company.

Entering our log house, we suddenly realized someone had been there, because a bountiful meal sat on our table. Neighbors, who lived about a mile away, had apparently seen the hearse pass their place earlier, and had prepared a variety of foods with much care. It was as if God were loving us through those thoughtful people. Their act of kindness brought a soothing to our hearts and a fresh assurance in our heavenly Father who would be our "Daddy" now during this profound loss.

Although bolstered by my faith at that time, insomnia was still a constant companion during the adjustment to widowhood and its relentless gnawing of grief. The loneliest hours after midnight in our hushed home seemed stuck in a time warp, hardly moving at all. I found myself hoping for Josiah's first squeaks of hunger. Then I could lift him out of his crib to feed him.

Josiah's hair was much lighter than his father's, but I could easily find features in our son's face that resembled Eddie. Anna, too, favored her "Daddy" in noticeable ways. Even as a toddler, that little girl was already exhibiting her father's innate concern for others. What priceless gifts Eddie had given our family!

After Josiah was fed, he would nestle comfortably against me and return to sleep. That was when I was able to slumber in our big easy chair, at least for a few hours.

While nights dragged on at a crawl, my days galloped by way too fast, because there was so much to do. Wilderness living was not easy, and it prevented us from seeing our friends very often.

Moreover, Eddie's family and mine lived thousands of miles away. Consequently, I soon learned how isolated we really were—and how hard my husband had worked to keep us all healthy and warm.

As mentioned, we lived "off the grid"—without conventional electricity—and I had no idea how to maintain our alternative power system. We also had a long, steep driveway to keep cleared of snow, a large yard to care for (in season), and a wood stove to stock for heating and cooking. In addition, our SUV needed to stay in good mechanical order. At the same time, I had two little ones to nurture. And now I found myself the sole supervisor of Emily's and Maria's homeschooling.

I was deeply grateful that my older daughters were already experts at cooking, at childcare, at cleaning, and even at administering natural treatments when needed. On the other hand, I admit I wasn't one of those super pioneer-type women who could expertly tackle all the chores in our wilderness abode and, simultaneously, care for each of her children's needs. I didn't even know how to run the gasoline-powered lawn mower.

One day out of the blue, Emily took me aside and declared, "Mama, I don't want you to get married again!"

I assured her that getting married, simply for a man to provide for us, was totally against my convictions. But I understood her concern, because our situation was difficult. *Anyway, who in his right mind would want to marry a woman with four children, two of which were so young?*

Then my eldest daughter demonstrated her maturity at only 13 years old when she revealed her awareness of my inadequacies: "Don't worry, Mama! I can do all the chores you cannot do."

With Maria helping with Anna and some of the cooking, Emily kept her word, applying all her mind and strength to the more "unseemly tasks." She picked up the cadavers and other smelly "gifts" our dogs brought to our doorstep. Then Emily would force a smile and praise our pets for their tokens of affection—a task I had no stomach for! After discreetly disposing of their offerings, she made kindling and split firewood. In fact, she mastered every outdoor skill needed around our home, except the falling and cutting of trees for our woodpile, because our chainsaw was broken. (I secretly claimed that a blessing, because I really didn't want my daughter to operate a dangerous chainsaw.)

But, Heavenly Father, how will we get the firewood we need?

God answered that prayer again and again, sometimes from the most unexpected sources. For example, some dear strangers we met at a store surprised us with a couple of loads of firewood one day. Missionary friends on furlough drove twelve hours one-way in order to help us with our wood supply.

When our situation again became desperate and we had no wood left for cooking or heating the next day, I drove to the post office, and while there, a friend from church pulled up in his truck. It was loaded with a chainsaw and other tools to suggest he was on his way to cut firewood somewhere.

When he asked how we were doing, I replied, "Fine."

His next question startled me: "Do you have any firewood?"

I simply said, "No."

Within a half-hour, that friend drove to our place. He cut down dead trees, then split enough wood to get us by for quite some time!

Over the ensuing months, as my children and I continued to heal, God also continued to demonstrate His marvelous, miraculous love for us by using others with big hearts and the willingness to do His bidding.

3

The Garment of Praise for the Spirit of Heaviness

CHAPTER 11

New Beginnings

One day while I drove, my older girls were whispering conspiratorially in the back seat. Then they sang out in unison, "Mama, we know the only man who would fit nicely into our family and who we would like!" (The twosome included Emily, who had told me only a few months before that she didn't want me to get married again!)

The children's earnest, orchestrated declaration took me totally by surprise. "Who?" I asked.

I could hear the smiles in their response: "Paul at church!"

I then smiled myself, because my daughters had noticed a true servant in the house of God, a true servant who was also a bachelor.

There must have been others thinking along the same lines, because whenever I needed a new visual aid built for the kindergarten Sabbath school class I taught, some of the women encouraged Paul Adams to assist me in the project. As he crafted those projects and helped in other various ways, we became friends. Then he began to join my children and me on nature hikes and other Sabbath afternoon activities. I was puzzled, however, because he never showed a sign of even knowing me when my children and I sat in church. In fact, it was like I didn't even exist in his mind!

Paul's odd behavior was confusing. "Lord," I prayed, "I can't deal with these ups and downs, not knowing where this friendship is heading. And I have no energy to invest emotionally in a relationship that's not according to Your will."

Then one Sabbath I offered another prayer, this one a "fleece" of sorts, uttered only in my thoughts. *Lord, if it's Your will for Paul and me to be together someday, please have him sit near me—here in church.* At the time, he was sitting clear away from my children and me on the other end of our pew.

Suddenly, I noticed Paul out of the corner of my eye. It looked like he had moved an inch or two toward us. Then during the service, I realized he was moving very slowly—inch by inch with pauses between toward our end of the long pew—until he was all the way over, sitting right beside us! (This slow-motion transit across the pew was not repeated until our commitment to each other was made known to the rest of our church family. And then, the transit was not so slow.)

My next private prayer took the form of another fleece: "Heavenly Father, if you intend for Paul and me to be together, will you, please, let me meet his mother?"

That very evening Paul's sweet mother came to the church, delivering a boy who was to stay with my children and me for a while. And that was when I was introduced to Paul's mom. *Thank you, God!*

Because our landlords now wanted to sell the beautiful log house that had served as our home for a year-and-a-half, my children and I needed another place to live.

I then placed a petition before God alone: "Heavenly Father," I prayed, "if it is Your will for Paul and me to be together, please impress him to ask me for courtship *before* the deadline when the children and I must move out of this house. I also ask You for a new place for us to live. . . . Dear Lord, if Paul doesn't ask me before that deadline, then the children and I will move back to Washington State. In Jesus' name, Amen!" (The day just before our deadline to move, Paul asked me for a "relationship with the intent toward marriage.")

During our courtship I learned much about Paul Adams and his stellar character. Several people in our church referred to Paul as a "gentle giant," because he was over six-feet tall. But he had also lived a quiet life in rural Montana with its towering mountains and pristine lakes and rivers.

Even when young, he had loved the outdoors where he could get away and just be in the quietude of a forest. Later, he became a gunsmith and worked as a millwright supervisor at a sawmill. Paul was not a hunter to kill animals, but he used the term as an excuse to get out in nature. Although somewhat shy, he learned early in life to serve others. Also, being devoted to his mother and having two younger sisters whom he dearly loved, Paul grew up treating females with deep respect.

Back when he gave his heart to the Lord, Paul found a local church and began to use his spiritual gift of "Helps." He was always ready to fix anything broken, solve other problems, and he even knew how to prepare a lot of food for fellowship meals. In addition, Paul was the sound-system man at church, a platform elder, an electrician, an usher, and so much more. Not only had he never married, but he had also lived 20 years without even a "girlfriend."

As the children and I prepared to move out of our log house, a woman in our church opened her home for my family. (Again, a homeowner had asked us to house-sit, although she knew some of my children were quite young.) Her trust warmed my heart as I watched my little Josiah and his sisters enjoy what to us was a mansion! After staying there a couple of months, another "spiritual sister" made her home available to us until Paul's and my wedding.

At Columbia Falls Seventh-day Adventist Church in February of 2003, two talented ladies decorated the sanctuary. They had crafted birch logs into tall candelabras to line the center aisle. Our dear friend, Melissa, had sewn my floor-length wedding gown and also red dresses in Swedish style for all three girls. Even little Josiah was dressed "special" for the occasion. (The children's outfits had all been a surprise for the bride!) Emily and Maria sang a duet for the ceremony. Then afterward, a reception lunch for about 170 guests completed the celebration.

In preparation for our lives together, God led us to a Montana mountain property with a hunting shack on it, a structure in much need of repair: no insulation, no foundation—just posts—single-pane windows, no indoor toilet or tub, and no running water. (We would have to fetch water from a nearby spring.)

Although Paul, the children, and I were experienced already in wilderness living, we would later learn that this property was just one more way of preparing us for mission service.

CHAPTER 12

Happy Hollow

Our hunter's shack was nestled into the side of a hollow between two hills. With large fir trees surrounding the cabin, it was bordered by a national forest on each side. In that hollow several springs watered a beautiful meadow.

Deprived of even an outhouse, we had to come up with a solution for waste disposal. Paul had heard somewhere from a military person that they sometimes disposed of waste by burning it. So Paul set up a large cooking pot (away from the house) and attempted to follow the military person's instructions, as he remembered them. The unsavory "stew" cooked all right. It just wouldn't disappear! And, meanwhile, I was hoping no visitor would wander onto our property and find my husband stirring the foul-smelling concoction.

We finally settled the dilemma by transporting an old outhouse to our property from that of Paul's parents. And after digging a pit, we no longer needed alternative methods.

Emily would mention from time to time how much she missed playing the "miracle piano," which had been in storage for months. Paul and I decided to save on the rental unit's cost by moving the piano into our cabin.

First, Paul built a plywood ramp for the back of his pickup truck, so we could push the piano from the storage unit into the truck bed.

Then we headed for our cabin. It was late that winter afternoon by the time Paul, Emily, Maria, and I arrived in front of our place. When Paul untied the rope holding the piano, the large instrument suddenly lurched out of the cargo bed and down the hill into deep snow, breaking off the lid!

Large snowflakes were sailing into the piano as darkness and cold descended all around us. Paul found another sheet of plywood and somehow managed to get the piano onto it. The poor instrument fell over again, this time onto its back.

We decided to leave the piano in that position on the plywood and try to push it up the steps onto the front porch. But we weren't able to move it more than three inches. That was when Paul suggested that we just leave it. But I couldn't bear the thought of our "miracle piano" buried in the snow as a discard.

Then Emily exclaimed, "Let's pray!"

As our daughter was fervently praying on her knees, Paul joined her in prayer to the "almighty and all-seeing God."

What happened next took my breath away. We again tried to push the piano up the steps. Suddenly, as if it were weightless, the piano almost lifted itself up the steps and onto the porch! And none of us felt the enormous weight as we had before. We then were able to maneuver it the rest of the way into our cabin. Apparently, angels of God had cared enough about a girl's prayer—and an old piano—to add their muscle to the task.

I stood there, surveying the large instrument, looking so forlorn with its broken keys and top lid ripped off. I couldn't help but wonder also about its strings after enduring Montana's extreme temperatures in that storage unit. Would it be horribly out of tune now, maybe impossible to tune? We would soon find out when the same piano tuner, who had fixed the piano before, made a house visit.

After driving through snow up the steep hill to our cabin, the piano tuner informed us he would never again come up a hill like that in winter. Sheepishly, I explained what had happened, and he began his work at once. Astonished, he said the instrument was still in tune. All he had to do was fix the broken parts, which after some time, he did.

That piano served our two older girls well and was such a blessing every time its sweet music wafted through our home.

With spring just around the corner, the cold mountain air and snow still lingered. After Paul erected a few pieces of plywood behind our cabin, we placed a bathtub inside the wood enclosure. Then a tarp for a roof created a cozy room for taking baths. Next, Paul added a 5-gallon bucket with a faucet underneath, along with a rope-and-pulley system—for a shower, too!

We fetched water from the spring in the middle of our 25-acre property. In winter, we headed out with a sled carrying several 5-gallon containers. Dipping them into the icy spring water, we would return to the cabin. Next, we heated that spring water on a small propane burner that also served as a heater for the "outdoor bathroom."

Eventually, we were able to build an indoor bathroom, and we turned the old rustic cabin into a cute country cottage. It took some imagination, paint, insulation, river rock, fabric, thread and needle. We also created a pond, catching water from one of the springs. We even kept horses, which really pleased our older daughters. It became a lovely place, surrounded in winters with blankets of pure white snow for sledding and cross-country skiing. Then in summers we would head out among the many wildflowers to pick huckleberries and explore endless trails.

The day arrived when we decided to sell our mountain cabin. God blessed, and our hard work brought a nice profit. Then we packed up our vehicle, and all six of us traveled east in search of a home that wouldn't need so much work—something completely finished, with electricity, running water, and indoor plumbing. This was not to be, however. We traveled all the way into the northern parts of Maine without any success in finding a suitable house. Meanwhile, another winter was coming on.

At that time, some friends from Montana contacted us more

than once, trying to convince us to return to their area and purchase their unfinished shell of a house. We finally decided to buy it, sight unseen, and we found ourselves "roughing it" once more.

God enabled us, again, to make something beautiful out of just a skeleton of a house. We were a good team, Paul and I. With great skill and much painstaking labor, he would follow my suggestions.

"Paul, let's make a pond!"

"Let's build a rock wall!"

"Let's make flowerbeds!"

As the months wore on, our new property took shape. But to serve self isn't satisfying, and soon a longing to do something more worthwhile was born within all of us.

CHAPTER 13

Call to Mission Service

Outside our Montana chalet-like home, wild rabbits scampered about, white daisies waved in a gentle breeze, bears ate clover, and down by the large pond, stately moose waded along the water's edge. Curious white-tailed deer would sniff around, too, always alert to movements within our log-sided house.

Indoors, a glowing fire chased away autumn's chill as Sabbath was about to begin. It had been a long day of preparation. Candles were lit in the chandelier, and each window reflected those flickering lights. A special traditional meal was already prepared, baths were over, clothing was ready for the morrow, and all was calm.

Snowcapped mountains slowly faded in the coming eve. Nineteen-year-old Emily, our "Gentle Dove," seated herself at the piano and enwrapped our home and hearts with melodic hymns. Then Maria, our "Squeaking Squaw," joined in with her violin. Her nickname bore no resemblance to the sound of her violin, however. Maria was "Squeaking Squaw" to us, because each time Mama or anyone else in the family tried to give her a smooch, she would emit a piercing shriek, and a wild chase would ensue. Then Papa, Mama, Anna (our "Babbling Brook"), and Josiah ("Chief Honey Bear") would all slip onto the sofa. The two younger children, now ages seven and six, would always be considered "our babies."

Everyone was ready for an evening of stories about missionary heroes braving jungles that teemed with wild animals and other dangers. Spellbound, my family would listen as I tried to make the words come to life. There was Eric B. Hare, the famous Australian missionary to the Karen people in Burma. He was known as "Doctor Rabbit," the "jungle nurse and storyteller." There were Mr. and Mrs. Cott and their adventures in South America; Ana and Ferdinand Stahl of the Peruvian Highlands; and so many more—great inspiration to welcome the Sabbath hours in our wilderness home.

Throughout the years, Emily had used these exciting stories as opportunities to persuade us as a family to commit ourselves to mission service. But that night she had a different subject on her mind, and she sounded profoundly sad. "I wonder where our horses are."

For days we had combed the mountains, knocked on many doors, and Maria had even circled over the valleys and hills in a friend's plane with the hope of sighting our beloved horses. But they had vanished. And when Anna's cats died, one after another, it appeared that the ties holding us most closely to our mountain home were unraveling, little by little.

Then Mike and Marilee Kier, missionaries from Thailand, shared their testimonies one Sabbath. Afterward, while standing in line for the fellowship meal, Mike Kier struck up a conversation with me.

"I used to want to be a missionary," I admitted to him, "but no longer."

"What happened to make you lose your desire to serve God in a foreign land?" he asked.

"We're too old, too tired, and I can't stand the heat, not even in Montana summers!" I exclaimed. Then I added, "Also, we're not a perfect family."

"Your youngsters don't need to be perfect," he said. "People just need to see that you're working with your children."

Mike Kier's simple counsel left me in deep thought about new possibilities for us. I had seriously believed we should stay in the mountains and "perfect" our characters before venturing out "to serve" in any major way. Now this missionary had reawakened a desire that had first gripped me at a young age, a desire to someday serve the poor on the other side of the planet, preferably in India.

Here we were, just ordinary people. But God must have known that He could use us despite our lack of "perfection," because from that day forward, it was as if every obstacle we encountered had automatic doors that immediately opened for us to sail through!

CHAPTER 14

India or Thailand?

When we told Paul's parents we believed God was leading us into mission service, they surprised us by saying, "We will sponsor you to begin with!"

Never did we expect such a positive response. Rather, we thought they would raise concerns. This was, once again, a sign we should keep going forward with our plans.

In my mind there was only one place for us, and that was India. And as events evolved, some missionaries in that country seemed genuinely interested in our family joining them—but not for another year.

Meanwhile, we ordered passports for each of us. As we searched for suitable training, every door shut. Then Wildwood Health Retreat in Tennessee was suggested. With my prior training as a Certified Nursing Assistant (CNA), I was drawn to an intensive medical missionary course offered by that health retreat—and so were Emily, Maria, and Paul. Moreover, my husband and I were especially impressed that even our younger children were welcome to join us at the Wildwood center. In addition, the price was affordable, the timing was perfect, and registration closed that very week!

We soon found ourselves in Tennessee for the specialized training. One of the instructors, Michael, showed slides from the

Thailand-Burma border during a few evening sessions. He and his wife had volunteered at the Lay Klo Yaw mission school there in Karen State on the Burma side of the border.

One day, Michael approached Paul and me privately, saying, "I think you should consider going to the Lay Klo Yaw school in Burma."

We replied almost in unison, "But we're going to India!"

Undaunted, Michael continued, "Please, pray about it, because I feel strongly that God is calling you to work among the Karen people at Lay Klo Yaw."

We told him we would pray, and several times a day, Paul and I kept our word with such prayers as, "Please, God, show us clearly what to do and where You want us to go. If it's Your will for us to change our plans for India and to serve at the Lay Klo Yaw school instead, please make it plain to us."

The following Sabbath, our family trooped into a church where we had never been before. And that very day in that very place we discovered details that caused us to realize our intended mission in India would not make a good match for our family.

Because my husband is quite levelheaded, not given to impulsive decisions, he had needed something concrete to convince him to give up our plans for India. Without any reservations in Paul's mind, he knew that door had just closed with a definite, "No!"

Michael smiled broadly when we informed him, "We're now willing to go to the Thailand-Burma border."

Within the next few months, providential events left no doubt that God was directing our every step. Because we'd been asked to work among the Karen people, I wanted to know all about them. That led me to research on the Internet and in books.

I learned that people of Karen descent are considered a "minority ethnic group," mainly living in the eastern part of Burma and the western part Thailand. Because of the constant warfare in Burma (also called Myanmar), many Karen dwelled in refugee camps that had sprung up along the border. Other Karen managed to survive in mountain and lowland villages, their income sources limited to small-scale agriculture and cottage-industry handicrafts.

The Karen are among the poorest in Thailand. Sadly, most of them remain stateless and can never benefit from citizenship. Therefore, they are unable to vote or participate in any industry that might better their lot. They can't even apply for a passport to travel elsewhere. Many of the border areas where they live are called "No Man's Land."

As I read more about the Karen, my heart swelled with sympathy for those forgotten people who had suffered much at the hands of the Burmese military.

While sitting at a classroom computer, I suddenly remembered we actually knew someone who was already a missionary along the Thai-Burma border. The young man's name was Dan; his family and ours had attended the same camp meeting each year. Then more recently, his mother had given me Dan's Web address, so I looked it up.

His website greeted me with several buttons. Thinking that one of those, labeled "People," would lead me to more details about the Karen, I found descriptions of teachers and other staff instead, including that of a "Pastor Jimmy." That pastor's name was one our instructor had mentioned.

"Michael!" I called. "This website has a 'Pastor Jimmy' on it."

When my instructor glanced at the computer screen, he surprised me with, "That's the Lay Klo Yaw mission school where you and Paul are headed!"

Our Asian mission adventure would soon begin, but not exactly as we had planned . . .

CHAPTER 15

A People Dear to Our Hearts

At long last, all six of us stepped onto Thai soil at Bangkok's Suvarnabhumi Airport

Shortly before departing on our venture, we were advised by people at our church's Thailand mission headquarters to avoid the Lay Klo Yaw school area—even the nearby villages. Apparently, when those directors actually saw our pictures and realized how tall and fair-haired we were, they knew we would draw unneeded attention and possible trouble, especially on the Burma side of the Moei River. But we had been quite sure of our call to that border. Now with the probable closing of that particular "door," however, we weren't as certain as before and began to wonder where exactly we should serve.

We shouldn't have worried about our eventual destination; it would soon become obvious that an unseen hand had already staked out each step of our journey.

After plodding through "Immigration" with our visas, then the baggage area, we were delighted to see Dan's familiar face. How grateful we felt for him to have traveled such a long way by bus to help us become familiar with this new country!

First, Paul and I presented Dan with a "care package" his mother had sent along with us. It was disguised as a well-packed suitcase.

Next, the young man led us to the nearest Automated Teller

Machine (ATM) and started our education regarding Thai baht bills and how ATMs would become the monetary lifeline for our mission.

Then he escorted all six of us through the airport concourse with its hodgepodge of travelers hurrying every which way. Leading us to a taxi queue, Dan helped us load most of our carry-ons and his luggage into the cab's ample trunk. Emily, Maria, Anna, Josiah, Dan, Paul, and I squeezed inside the taxi for an exciting ride through the most chaotic traffic I'd seen since Calcutta, India, many years before! Although a bit cramped, we all did survive the thrilling ride to the hotel Dan had recommended for the night.

Clean and somewhat rested the next morning, our family got our exercise as we tried to keep up with Dan's fast pace. He found us some sidewalk tables where we could order breakfast of stir-fry and rice.

Then Dan walked us to a shop where we could purchase a cell phone, another "lifeline" for our mission (wherever that would be).

After retrieving our luggage at the hotel, we all loaded into a taxi once again, this time through the bustling streets of Bangkok to the bus station. (Not only was this the largest city in Thailand, it was also one of the largest in all of Southeast Asia.)

As I gripped the armrest beside me, I listened to Dan chat in a singsong language with the taxi driver. For such a young American man, Dan had proved extraordinary as a hospitable host for each person in our family during our brief stay in this amazing city.

We couldn't thank him enough when we later boarded a bus to Mike and Marilee Kier's mission post about an hour's trip north of Bangkok. (Dan would later take an overnight bus plus a few more smaller modes of transportation back to the Thai-Burma border.)

Ever since Mike Kier had spoken with me at our Montana church's fellowship dinner, both he and his wife Marilee had kept in contact, encouraging us in our quest for a mission post. And now here they were at a bus stop, all smiles and welcoming—tall Mike with Marilee who barely reached her husband's chin when she stood on tiptoes.

Before coming to the bus stop, the Kiers had visited a Thai mini-market and bought us a bag of different vegetarian packaged foods, so we would have an idea of what was available for us in our new environment. But their best gift was that of rest and nourishing meals during the few days we stayed with them. After all, they knew from experience how exhausted we would be after traveling through several time zones and maneuvering through Bangkok.

By the time they transported us to the train station for our long journey to Chiang Mai, all six of us were rested and ready. I couldn't help but shed a few tears when we hugged the Kiers goodbye. These dear missionaries had been such a positive influence in our taking this "leap of faith" to an Asian country.

We soon found that train travel was much easier on us than the cramped seats in a plane, bus, or taxi. Now even the little ones had space to move more freely, and that helped encourage more pleasant dispositions during the lengthy trip.

At Chiang Mai a "retired" Karen minister greeted us. Then he loaded our family and all our carry-ons into his vehicle for a trip to a venue many hours north of Chiang Mai. There the minister conducted a ten-day, well-attended health seminar.

I would later realize how important that training was, especially from a Karen pastor whose lectures were flavored with Karen culture and other nuances vital in our future ministry among those special people.

After the seminar ended and we returned to the pastor's center in Chiang Mai, our friend Dan phoned us.

"Momo Susanna wants all of you to visit her here at Lay Klo Yaw," he said. "How soon can you come?"

I thought at once about the church's leadership warning us not to settle at the Lay Klo Yaw school because of our physical appearances drawing possible danger. Susanna was a long-ago acquaintance of mine, however, and I felt my heart winning over the warning. Anyway, our visit would be short.

After conferring with Paul, I phoned Dan back, assuring him that we would be happy to travel to Lay Klo Yaw. He then told us which bus to take from Chiang Mai to Mae Sariang where he would meet us. From there he would advise us on what conveyances to take along the way to the border.

As promised, Dan again came to our aid, meeting us at Mae Sariang, three hours from our destination. I looked over at our friend who was untying a large, well-protected bundle of bedding from his motorcycle. He had been riding his motorcycle through a downpour, so his drenched clothing hung limply on his tall body. My only solace seeing Dan in such a state was the warm temperature that prevented any chill. Also comforting was knowing that the young man would be following us on his motorcycle.

Riding in the back of a small pickup truck called a *songthaew*, we were heading into a more intriguing place. The roads became winding with sharper curves as we left the hills and headed into steep and rugged mountains. We eventually drew closer to the border. The Moei River came into view far below, and it looked to me like a long, squiggly stream of light chocolate milk.

Dan directed us to a small border village, and I suddenly realized that although we were still in Thailand, we had come upon a completely different world and culture than America, Sweden—or even Thai cities! We might as well have entered a new country and stepped years back in time.

We had arrived on the border separating Thailand from Karen State, Burma, and many of the inhabitants there on the Thai side were Karen. They didn't speak Thai, nor did they dress in modern Thai clothing. In fact, everything about these people was different, from the way they dressed to the way they greeted others with only a nod.

Not much happened without our notice. The older women, with towels wrapped around their heads like turbans, chewed betel nut and welcomed us with huge toothless grins. (Or, perhaps, they just found our own dress and features amusing. Whatever the case, all of us—including young Anna and Josiah—smiled warmly back at them.)

It was almost dusk when we were motioned into the back of another pickup truck. After a 30-minute ride, we all headed to the river in a downpour. It became clear to Paul, Emily, Maria, and me that this river crossing was to be made quietly and without our being seen. We were then ushered down a path of slimy mud.

Our first experience in the low-slung canoe across the muddy Moei caused some apprehension on my part, especially concerning Anna and Josiah's safety. The engine coughed, then started with a roar, and off we went through the equally roaring river. But we made it to the other side without any problems.

Trudging up Burma's slippery shore, we stood in Karen State, beautiful Kaw Thoo Lei, meaning "The Land without Darkness and Evil." At once I spotted Susanna sliding down the path toward us. She hugged Emily, Maria, and me with great gusto and led us all up to the Lay Klo Yaw mission school. Susanna's loving exuberance chased away any residual anxiety, and it easily explained how she had so quickly earned her title of *Momo,* "Mother" to the staff and students.

We older ones in the family hauled the six carry-ons. Then Dan pointed to a nearby bamboo hut, handed us the plastic-covered pillows and blankets he'd brought, then told us with a grin, "Make yourselves at home!"

And we did just that as we placed the bedding inside our hut. Carefully opening the plastic, we found sleeping mats, then spread them out on the floor. Because we were advised to hang the enclosed mosquito nets while there was still enough light, we took care of that chore, also. Then we tucked each net securely around the mats. A few minutes later, we were invited to another bamboo hut to sit and partake of a simple meal of rice and small dishes of vegetables placed before us on the bamboo floor.

While eating, we heard the sound of distant artillery fire, and I cringed. But Susanna assured us that Karen soldiers were on guard day and night. Then she pointed to their eerie lights flickering back and forth along the darkening riverbank.

"Anyway," she said, "since the start of rainy season, the Burmese army has stayed pretty much stationary. Only once in a while, do they sound off artillery to keep the Karen on notice that they are coming—eventually."

Soon our family joined the entire Lay Klo Yaw student body and staff in their worship hour. I felt as if we were experiencing a sampling of Heaven when well over a hundred child voices sang about Jesus with all their hearts. Then individual students, from old to young, prayed with the same kind of fervor. I was amazed especially at the earnest praise and petitions of such young people, although our own children had learned to pray earnestly at a young age as well.

After sleeping for the first time on the traditional mats under the protective nets in our guest hut, we were greeted early with more singing from young voices as the students made their way to a large bamboo building where they all crowded in to sing some more, pray, then listen intently to a Bible story. After morning worship and breakfast, our own Maria shocked Paul and me with a request.

Back in Montana, Maria had been the only reluctant one in our family about flying off to Thailand, because it meant giving up her longtime dream of becoming a bush pilot in Alaska or South America. Now she informed us that this was her place of service, there at that mission school. Her desire was confirmed when we heard that the kindergarten teacher had just taken medical leave. So the school was in need of a teacher for the kindergartners.

Paul and I retreated privately to our hut and made Maria's request a serious matter of prayer. Then we discussed the situation, especially the fact that Burma was in the midst of an on-again-off-again decades-long war. Susanna had told us that the school should receive warning in plenty of time if the Burmese were to attack.

Eventually, it was settled. Our Maria would stay at Lay Klo Yaw and teach 45 lively kindergartners. I knew our daughter would take her responsibility seriously and do an excellent job. After all, she'd been a good student herself—and in training for years by helping educate her own younger siblings in many ways. But when we hugged her goodbye at the river's edge, I choked back tears.

Maria's excitement was visible. She was eager to teach those youngsters whom she had heard earnestly singing and praying the night before and that very morning. At only 17 years old, our daughter was ready to get started on her job and serve the remainder of that school year.

I quickly realized during that brief time in Karen State, Burma, at the Lay Klo Yaw school, a love was born for the Karen people, a love in all of us, fueled by their great need in that war-torn land. Our instructor, Michael, back at the Wildwood center in Tennessee, was right. At least one of us was supposed to serve at Lay Klo Yaw. And Paul, Emily, and I hoped that we, too, could find a ministry to those precious Karen, at least on the Thai side of the Moei River.

Emily was the next among the rest of us in the family to learn of a place for her to serve the Lord. To reach her assignment, we drove off the main road along the border and headed up into the mountains where we found a quaint village with a Thai government school for the "Thai Mountain Karen." The village chief was a Seventh-day Adventist, and he asked Emily to stay in his home with his family.

Although Emily enjoyed her time in the chief's home and in teaching the Karen children through the rest of the school year in the Thai mountains, she felt another place tugging at her heart. It was the mountains in Burma where the most horrific crimes against humanity were perpetrated; where land mines were planted by both friend and foe; and where the ever-present, decades-long civil war played its ugly game of life and death. That was the place for which her heart yearned.

"Mama, I know that one day God is going to call me to work there," Emily said. I tried not to show my true feelings and held my tongue. After all, at 20 years old, our eldest daughter was entering adulthood. She was sensible, a hard worker, and wholly devoted to God.

Since Emily had found her niche for now, Paul and I both wondered where the Lord wanted us to minister (with Anna and Josiah). Seeking the advice of a respected Karen pastor, we told him that although we were open to serving God anywhere, the Karen people had already captured our hearts, and our desire was to work among them.

After seeking prayerful counsel, the advisors suggested we go ahead and find housing close to Lay Klo Yaw, but on the Thai side of the border. That way we would live near enough to our daughters in case they needed our help.

Their counsel fit neatly into our original ideas about our family living among or near the populace for about a year. Not only did we want to minister in some way to our neighbors, but a dream was already beginning to form, a dream of eventually launching some sort of small children's home for orphans.

A couple of Adventist gentlemen escorted us to several different houses for us to consider to rent or buy on the Thai side of the Moei River. But none of the houses appealed to us. Therefore, we apologized to the nice men and asked for a few more days to pray and to look around on our own.

Before departing that area, Paul and I walked with Anna and Josiah to a small open-air restaurant in one of the nearby villages. I used a Thai-language dictionary to ask the owner if she knew of a house for rent. Suddenly, I heard an English-speaking Thai man translating for me. Then he translated her response into English: "Yes, I do! And I will take you there right now."

When we saw the old wooden house on posts nestled in long, overgrown grass with lots of (lime) fruit trees nearby, we knew at once this was the place for us. At the time, we mistakenly assumed its somewhat remote location would give us privacy to work with our younger children as we continued homeschooling them. Also, we would be within walking distance of several villages and, best of all, close to the river crossing to the Lay Klo Yaw school.

The wooden house had been vacant for over ten years and needed much attention, which was promised—if we would simply commit to renting the house for an entire year. With our own funds and with Paul's parents already supporting our ministry, we were able to pay the full amount, and the commitment was made.

The goodness of the Lord is phenomenal. He knew exactly what we needed. And He had a plan and a work for us in that very place, a plan we could never have imagined.

CHAPTER 16

Fears

Soon we were settled among the Karen people in our 600-square-foot wooden house. The landlady had kept her word and hired workers to clean the place, inside and out. Then she hired carpenters for necessary repairs and remodeling.

With enough electricity to power overhead light bulbs and with actual single-pane glass for windows, we looked upon our new abode as a genuine blessing—especially with a two-burner propane stovetop in the kitchen! One thing I objected to at once, however, was the metal bars installed over the windows, so Paul quickly and permanently removed them.

When Emily and Maria later visited our rustic "new" home, they were appalled by the sharp contrast between our house and the traditional bamboo huts of nearby villages. They felt embarrassed by that contrast, and they made it known to us that they hoped we all could someday live in a bamboo hut like many of our neighbors.

With the help of a translator, we quickly came to realize that those neighbors in nearby villages were often ruled by fears. They were afraid to go to a hospital, not because of possible pain. Even Karen children are quite stoic, bravely enduring all kinds of medical procedures without a fuss. Traveling to a hospital, however, meant passing through several soldier and police checkpoints. They feared being jailed in Thailand, then possibly being shipped to Burma.

Other fears involved the "spirit world." Ghosts and demons are very real to the Karen. For that reason, even big, brawny men are afraid of the dark. Some Karen parents teach their children to behave by threatening them: "If you're naughty, the spirits will come and get you!"

Many of the Karen perform rituals to appease the spirits, and they keep spirit altars in their homes and businesses. In Thailand they "feed the spirits" anything they believe would make the spirits happy. Moreover, the lives of these precious people are ruled by numerous superstitions regarding birth, water, smoke, rain, seasons, the washing of hair and laundry, and the handling of dead bodies.

Sadly, even Karen Christians can struggle with fears like these. Those who are not mature in their faith sometimes succumb to a constant fear of "displeasing the spirits."

Adding to all that fear is the genuine danger of disease. Almost every person we've talked with in our area has lost at least one child to malaria, dysentery, pneumonia, or fevers.

Like many dwellings in Thailand, the home we rented came with a "spirit house." We tried to explain to our landlord via a translator, "We don't need the spirit house. We worship the one and only God, the God of Heaven and Earth. He will protect us."

The landlord looked horrified and sounded quite concerned when she exclaimed, "But the spirits will look over your property and keep you safe." (As she spoke, I noticed the property's caretaker eavesdropping on our conversation.)

When we returned to finish moving into our rental home, the spirit house had mysteriously disappeared. Under closer scrutiny, Paul and I found it in pieces down the steep hill to a creek. Later, we learned that the Karen caretaker had decided to dispose of the spirit house for us. He proudly announced he was not afraid of the spirits; he was a Buddhist, but not an animist spirit-worshiper like many Buddhists in Thailand were.

Eric B. Hare, a long-ago missionary, mentioned in one of his books that God brought him and his wife to serve among the Karen people, who in his days, were "spirit-worshipers." Now we were discovering that the worship of spirits still remained after all those years.

"You are not safe in this house!" Those translated words pelted us from every direction. Furthermore, we were told more than once, "It's dangerous to live all by yourselves outside the village." Others warned, "You will be robbed, kidnapped, or murdered!"

We always replied with confidence, "God has clearly directed us to this house and area, and we're already committed to stay here for a year."

Meanwhile, the man whom our landlady had asked to be our groundskeeper, kept taking it upon himself to act as our guard. He insisted we close the bamboo gate each time we left and asked us to tie up the propane tank with a chain; he also told us to put anything valuable into the outdoor toilet and to lock the door to the house.

"Paul," I complained, "I refuse to live as if everyone is my enemy. I've read stories of missionaries living with guards and high fences and locked gates. If we pattern our lives like that, then we might as well return to America!" Come to think of it, even in America we left our door unlocked—even when gone for months. Also, I often left my purse in the unlocked truck in our driveway.

Our refusing to abide by the gardener's guidelines really upset the man. Although I felt sorry for him, we wanted our new neighbors to feel welcome. Therefore, we never locked the door nor closed the gate.

But someone else was lying awake at night because of fear— our landlady. Living on the river property across the road, she later informed us (again, through a translator), "I cannot sleep at night, because I keep listening and worrying about your safety."

With all those warnings, I found my own mind and faith beginning to waver. I, too, would awaken at night to the slightest noise, then nudge my poor husband. "Paul . . . what was that?"

Once in a while, the sounds were guns and land-mine explosions in the far distance on the Burma side of the river. Or closer, villagers would come right onto our porch and hunt Tokay lizards. Then those nighttime hunters would sell the prized reptiles. (Actually, we admired our neighbors' entrepreneurial spirit!)

Not too long after we rented the house near the lime orchard, we looked for a dependable means of transportation. Checking advertisements in English, we found a "crew cab" type truck with a roomy bed (for extra passengers), and its motor had recently been rebuilt. One feature I wasn't excited about was the phrase, "gold color." With the poverty in our area, I would feel self-conscious, driving through nearby villages in a "gold chariot." But that concern instantly vanished when we inspected the vehicle. The gold had faded to a bland color that was further decorated in patches of rust. Thus, we nicknamed our vehicle, "Old Trusty Rusty"!

Sometimes all four of us would climb into Old Trusty Rusty and head for Chiang Mai, the northern-most large city in Thailand, a seven-hour drive. Our vehicle would labor up, up, then over the mountains along Burma's border, those rugged heights reminding me of the Rocky Mountains we had left behind. I kept thinking of all the thousands of Thai and Karen villagers in those mountains, who didn't yet know God. And I hoped we could help at least some of those people learn about His wonderful gospel and also help them in other ways.

The first time we visited Chiang Mai, I admit to disappointment. It was just a "cement jungle" to me. But after a few more visits, we began to see what we were blind to at first. After all, Chiang Mai was the easiest option for quality medical care and for obtaining certain supplies for our mission. It now seems quaint and even somewhat romantic to our eyes.

Although the ancient city wall was crumbled, it was still there, also the mote around the city center, fountains, a myriad of guesthouses, and charming restaurants with lots of vegetarian options. We never have made an effort to visit Buddhist temples, but those many temples were an excellent reminder of *why* we were in Thailand.

A seasoned missionary took us to a few tourist places in Chiang Mai: The Tiger Kingdom, The Elephant Show, and Orchid Gardens. He also told us about the amazing zip lines, dirt bike trails, and rafting opportunities.

Once when the four of us were in Chiang Mai for medical needs, it was time to return to our house on the border. We had slept well at a guesthouse, so well that my mind rebelled against the very thought of leaving. It had felt so good to sleep without being surrounded by so much fear.

When I picked up my Bible, I happened to open it to Acts 18; and to my dismay, verses 9 and 10 were highlighted with a heavenly glow. *And the Lord said to Paul in the night by a vision, "Do not be afraid any longer, but go on speaking and do not be silent; ¹⁰ for I am with you, and no man will attack you in order to harm you, for I have many people in this city."*

Without an inkling of doubt, I knew God had spoken. The glow around the verses was too bright not to be from Him. And His command was clear, "Go back! I have many people there. Do not fear . . ." And best of all, God promised to be with us!

When we returned to the border, my fear had fled—and just in time. Soon, the sounds of war would reverberate among the mountains and we would become involved in helping evacuate the mission school across the Moei. But long before the evacuation of Lay Klo Yaw, our desire was to find a piece of land to use as a family ministry. We still dreamed of having a small home for displaced children. (We had already visited orphanages throughout Thailand and even into Cambodia, hoping to learn from those examples.)

Eh K'Nyaw took us to some places, looking for property for our children's home. But right next to our own rented wooden house grew a lime orchard. (Apparently, the local Thai residents didn't differentiate between limes and lemons, because the orchard was called Beh Noe Gleh Glaw, meaning, The Lemon Garden.) As we overlooked it from our porch, we could see the creek, the orchard, and we could even hear bells tinkling on the grazing goats beyond.

Imagining the lime orchard (or The Lemon Garden) would make the most peaceful and perfect site for the children's home, I prayed, *Lord, this is the place . . .* (or so I thought).

Soon we received the discouraging news that the orchard was already sold. A young missionary from Norway, a man of another Christian faith, had just purchased the orchard for a children's home and vocational training school—much like our own intentions.

Then about that time, the land across the nearby quiet highway was offered to us and, of course, we would have loved to own that fantastic property. But the price was way out of the question.

When we later found ourselves responsible for the whole school of 120 children, Paul and I again prayed together at the edge of the lime orchard prior to leaving for America, "Lord Jesus, if it be Your will, please have the owner sell the lime orchard property to us; please make something happen that will bring that to reality, but, again, only according to Your will."

The very long flight for our much-needed furlough in the United States was drawing to a close. And so ended my reverie that had paused only for meals and naps along our way above the Pacific.

Back to the reality of stiff joints and groggy children, Paul and I put away coloring books, crayons, and other items. Before long, we lifted our carry-ons and joined others in the aisle for passage out of the plane and into Portland International Airport. Paul's parents were there to greet us; then after a good overnight rest, we piled into our old Suburban and traveled to Montana.

Going from the heat and humidity of Thailand to the cool climate of Montana was a "culture shock" in reverse. Also, we noticed at once how American prosperity and conveniences were unequivocally poles apart from the poverty surrounding us on the Thai-Burma border.

Still, the wilderness home of Paul's parents was more in line with what we all were used to, at least in America. Meanwhile, as we enjoyed the serenity of Montana's mountains and rivers, we truly began to relax and obtain the rest and refurbishment we needed for our bodies and minds.

Furloughs were never truly relaxing, though. Between frequent communications with those at our school, traveling far and near for speaking engagements regarding our mission, and even traveling from Montana to Arizona's hot desert for an ASI (Adventist Laymen's Services and Industries) convention, we kept busy.

CHAPTER 17

Miracle of the Lime Orchard

During our furlough in the United States, something sinister invaded the mountain retreat center where the Lay Klo Yaw students and staff were living and studying at the temporary boarding school. The invasion was part of the age-old war between good and evil, between Christ and Satan, in the form of demonic harassment. Add a theft to the mix, and the situation quickly mushroomed.

Various biblical measures were taken, but some of the students were gravely affected, and to maintain peace, they needed to be separated from the other students. Meanwhile, Gayle, Eh K'Nyaw, and Emily were consulting with Paul and me by phone.

I then recalled the animist "spirit altars" we had discovered on that property back when we were desperate for a temporary location for the students. We had taken down some of the altars and had, simply, covered up the rest. All the while, however, at least a few of the grounds' caretakers were animists and may have been currently using those altars as part of their rituals. If that were the case, then the evil one would have acquired a "legal foothold" on that wonderful refuge and was behind the harassment among some of our students.

While consulting with Gayle and staff, we unanimously agreed that all the children should be moved from the mountain retreat center as quickly as possible. But every prospective property would not become available soon enough.

Meanwhile, Paul and I felt strongly impressed to ask the staff at the school to set aside two or three days in special prayer for a property "of God's choice" to become immediately accessible.

After praying for an hour about that need, Eh K'Nyaw left the retreat center and ventured down the mountain. When he reached a village near the Moei River, a man on a motorbike approached him and said, "The lemon orchard is for sale!"

When Eh K'Nyaw phoned us about this possible new development, we asked him to go visit the orchard's owner, Ole, the young Norwegian missionary who had purchased that land. We also asked Eh K'Nyaw to tell Ole that Paul and I would phone him that evening, "Thailand time."

When we called Ole later, he told us that no one knew he had need of funds for another project. And if the orchard's sale would provide the needed funds for his new project to be launched—and if we really needed that property for our students—then, yes! He would sell it to us.

Both Paul and I held our breath upon asking the price. Ole said he would sell the lime orchard property for the same price he had paid for it, $20,000. (And that happened to be the exact amount remaining in Paul's retirement savings!) Our hearts soared even higher when Ole added, "You can move the children there tomorrow, if you like. And you can wait to pay me until you return to Thailand."

This missionary was truly open to the Holy Spirit, and we could sense his sincere kindness—even from a phone half a world away!

Not surprising, when the children moved from the mountain property to the lime orchard, all demon harassment ended immediately.

Our staff and the older teenagers worked fast at fixing up the orchard's wooden building earmarked for a temporary girls' dormitory. There was also a very old bamboo structure that was missing most of its roof. But several blue tarps stretched over its top made that building habitable for the boys' dorm. In just three days the staff and teenage students also erected modest bamboo huts for staff "living quarters." Then they all added a bathroom, and even created a suitable pole building for preparing meals. We were told that our new "school" looked a little sparse, but it was a good beginning. Moreover, the teenage boys were already planning to construct two much larger bamboo dormitories, a long one for the girls and a two-story structure for the boys.

Upon returning from furlough and with renewed visas in hand, Paul and I were overcome with emotion at how wondrously God had intervened with the lime orchard purchase. But this euphoria was short-lived, because authorities sought another solution to our situation. They wanted to take us across the Moei River to Karen State, Burma, in hopes of convincing us to restart our school over there. It would be close to the site of the former Lay Klo Yaw mission school that the Burmese army had destroyed.

The new school would be protected by the DKBA, the Democratic Karen Buddhist Army, which at that time was working under the Burmese army.

Therefore, Paul and I, along with Emily, Gayle, and a few school staff members who would also serve as interpreters, joined government and military officials in canoes and crossed the Moei River to the Burma shore. We were aghast to see among the military there to greet us, child soldiers, armed and in full uniform!

Then they led us to the area where they wanted us to build the new school. (A huge bulldozer had cleared away the land mines.)

"And now the grounds are safe," they assured us.

As Paul and I gazed at the nearby charred remains of the Lay Klo Yaw mission school, we felt profound grief. And that grief was at stark odds with being asked to pose for pictures of this "historic event" with both Thai officials and the Burmese military.

The officials explained that we, indeed, could build the school and bring all the children back across the river. Then Paul and I would be allowed to live there and manage the campus. But the array of uniforms mixed with the ceremonial event reminded us of recent troubles concerning our lime orchard: some of the Thai soldiers, who had shelters on a hill overlooking the girls' temporary dormitory in the orchard, would become intoxicated. Those soldiers would even sneak onto our property at night in hopes of befriending the young ladies in the dorm. This traumatized the girls and caused great concern among our staff.

With those incidents in mind, I asked the leader of the DKBA if our girls would be guaranteed safety and not be bothered by the many soldiers in the area.

I took the leader's delayed reply—and his avoidance to look squarely into my eyes when he spoke—as a strong warning not to go forward with his proposal. Besides, after the extraordinary purchase of the lime orchard, Paul and I knew God had a different plan for our school—a much better plan.

4

That they Might be Called Trees of Righteousness

CHAPTER 18

Porch Patients

After politely turning down the officials' offer for us to rebuild the Lay Klo Yaw school across the river, Paul and I felt a greater urge to search for a way to convince the Thai government to allow us to keep the children on our side of the Moei.

We prayed, "What would You have us do, Lord?" Then we sought advice from various individuals. But everyone replied, "It's impossible!"

Next, we contacted our personal "encouragement team," Mike and Marilee Kier, because we knew they would take our problem to the Lord in earnest prayer and then give us a well-thought-out answer, which they did:

"We have a friend who has a Thai foundation, and she is willing to try to help you."

This woman of another Christian faith traveled many hours to reach our area. Then she spent many more hours interceding on our behalf with government officials and local soldiers. Her sweet, humble, faith-filled persistence won their hearts; and within a short time, we knew God Himself was intervening. Through this woman, the Lord touched the officials in a special way.

We came to believe those men were placed in their positions at that time for a purpose. Their courtesy toward the children and us touched *our* hearts, too. Then with much military and government display and ceremonies, we at last gained permission to keep the children under the Thai woman's foundation and, thus, to remain at our facility.

With this miraculous intervention, Paul and I finally discovered our true mission in this land of very needy people. First, there were the many students from the Lay Klo Yaw school on the other side of the river which we renamed "Sunshine Orchard Learning Center" on our side of the Moei. Next, after word spread of our ministry to these children, which included providing for their medical needs, people began to bring us orphans and other children who were sick. Some of those little ones became the nucleus of our family's "small children's home," the one Paul and I had envisioned at the onset of our foreign ministry.

Ningeh was our first baby, arriving a little before the others. His mother, an alcoholic, brought him to us. Both our older daughters happened to be home at the same time. In fact, Maria had just returned from America. And now she was a bona fide emergency medical technician (EMT).

I remember how horrible little Ningeh smelled. His stench was so intense that Emily decided to give the little guy a bath before Maria could examine him properly. Emily told us later how amazed she was to find a clean baby emerge out of such filthy water—and how surprised to find that Ningeh actually enjoyed the bath! Even today, baths are Ningeh's favorite pastime.

Because the child's poor mother had no milk of her own to feed him, we gave her formula, which we later learned she immediately traded for alcohol. Over time, we took Ningeh to the hospital with measles and for many other ailments.

One sad day Ningeh's mother appeared on our doorstep when her son was eight months old. Skin and bones, the baby couldn't even hold up his head. In that moment, we realized he wouldn't survive unless his mother allowed us to take him.

"Please, let us make him well," I pleaded.

Ningeh's mother eventually agreed for us to care for him until he was two years old. (And by God's grace, we still have him today.)

As soon as the mother left, Maria scooped up the baby and was on her way to the hospital at Mae Tan, about two hours away. There he was admitted.

After five days of a doctor's expertise and Maria's constant care, the child emerged from the hospital in much better health. Tragically, though, Ningeh's mother later died while out in the fields, foraging for edibles.

Next to arrive was little Juju. Her mother had died of a bowel obstruction. This family had recently accepted Jesus into their lives, and now a sorrowful husband placed nine-month-old Juju in our care.

Not long thereafter, relatives arrived with Juju's two siblings, three-year-old Moawah and five-year-old Saw Kwe Leh. When little Moawah entered our home, it was with the air of a petite queen with curly dark hair. And in no time, she won our hearts. Her older brother Saw Kwe Leh, with his doe-like eyes, would try his best to obey despite our language barrier. He easily endeared himself to us as well.

Next, Moawah and Saw Kwe Leh were joined by a cousin, a true orphan raised by her aunt. Thus, six-year-old Memewah also slipped into our growing family.

We soon became quite busy caring for little ones. Moreover, our evenings stretched long as we continued to treat students' scabies, ringworm, and various injuries. Often, too, we kept those sick with malaria through the night. Then morning light would come with villagers already on our porch in need of medical help. Other duties also mounted, such as fetching water for the school, buying supplies, printing teachers' papers and exams, preparing worships, and so many other activities.

Throughout this initial buildup of our ministry among the Karen people, Eh K'Nyaw was a lifesaver. He was gifted with the ability to open God's Word to the students and to minister to villagers as well. In addition, Eh K'Nyaw often served as our translator, truly a blessing to us!

Our porch continued as a medical focal point for the villagers as Gayle Haberkam faithfully tended to their needs just outside our front room. Always open to God's leading, however, she began to find other needs in far-off places. Then one day our American friend, Dan, showed up unexpectedly and took Gayle to the Thai mountain village where he used to teach English. Although the village was extremely remote, Gayle felt a new calling, one that would also reach other mountain tribes. Because of their isolation, these people had even less of a chance for survival in cases of serious sickness or accident than those coming to us for help. And how could I complain about losing Gayle when there were hundreds of mountain villages without any medical care—and without any Christians like Gayle who lived the gospel everywhere she traveled?

Cold season, hot season, and rainy season had all come and gone. And now Maria was gone, too. She was traveling to a medical missionary training seminar north of Chiang Mai. Apparently, word spread quickly of Gayle's and Maria's absence, because our porch "clinic" temporarily became fairly quiet.

To be honest, I enjoyed having the porch sometimes for just my new little children and for the students, not needing to worry about betel nut spit and babies with no diapers and the resulting contamination. Our students still had medical needs, and our porch remained the place to doctor them all. I admit, though, to cringing when strangers with a myriad of illnesses mingled with the vulnerable little children now in our family.

One morning a woman, diagnosed with tuberculosis (TB), spit betel nut juice on the ground outside our home; then the children's freshly washed laundry, hanging to dry on the porch railing, fell down, landing in the spit. It was more than I could take, but by the grace of God, I kept quiet.

Another woman was sitting nonchalantly in a puddle of her baby's urine. Then an emaciated-looking man arrived, also with the symptoms of TB. He produced a small plastic bag from his soiled pants pocket and carefully started to untie the string around the bag, to show me the bloody, yellow mucous. I quickly asked my translator for that day to inform him there was no need for me to see it. I already knew what it was. And I also noted that he wore no facemask and had nothing but his hands and clothing to wipe his mouth after coughing up more phlegm. To make matters worse, he was chewing betel nut and, thus, would probably spit even more!

With Paul away on business, Emily offered to care for our little ones that day while I took the man to the hospital at Mae Sot. Upon arrival, the medical aide immediately placed a facemask over the patient's mouth and nose. Then scolding with a clucking sound, he ushered the man out of the hospital, forbidding him to enter through the usual waiting area. Taking our places among the other banished sick ones outside, we waited our turn.

Dear Father, I silently prayed, *how can I keep myself from making our patients feel ostracized—as if they were lepers—when they come to our home? They haven't a clue about germs and contamination.*

I recall once during our early days in Thailand, when villagers with health problems arrived while we were eating lunch, and Paul was not around. We felt we couldn't be inhospitable and eat without inviting them to join us. So we served them food on a floor mat where we all sat down in a circle. Each person was given a plate of rice. Smaller bowls of various vegetables, with a serving spoon in each, surrounded the large bowl of rice. I wasn't accustomed to the way they took the serving spoon from each dish, sipping from that spoon, then dipping it into the next dish—to the mouth and back. Many of their teeth were rotten and rimmed in red from betel nut juice. Also, most of those lunch guests were there because of some illness. I felt anxious about contamination, not sure of what to do.

Then Paul returned, washed his hands, and proceeded to join us on the floor around our meal. Becoming somewhat frantic, I tried to signal him privately about the danger of germs swimming around in the serving bowls. But he looked clueless and served himself a portion from every single bowl. All I could do was bite my tongue and pray in silence.

Later we learned to serve our guests each a plate, complete with the rice, curry sauce, and various vegetables. (No longer does it bother me to eat together like that, not even to share a cup. But we avoid the latter if we know the people are ill.)

As soon as the news spread that our Maria had returned to our house, the villagers arrived in droves. They reminded me of the multitudes who came to Jesus, pressing in on Him, hoping to be healed. To love as Christ loved while here on Earth is our constant aim. He is our example, but we had much to learn.

Jesus exuded compassion for the multitudes. He pitied their sad condition. He didn't think of self and wasn't afraid of contamination. He touched the untouchable, He healed in season and out of season. The welfare of those people was His focus. And because the multitudes thronged around Jesus, He found little time to rest. Therefore, we thanked God for our "porch patients" and for Jesus' example in showing us how to love, not only with words, but also with actions.

We truly do love these poor, neglected people, and would rather have them come to us than not. But I must admit to a daily struggle to surrender my growing family's and my needs when people showed up at six o'clock in the morning.

Maria also loved our "porch patients," but like Gayle Haberkam, our daughter was beginning to feel a greater burden for the isolated villagers way up in Thailand's remote mountains. The day she ventured out on her recently purchased motorcycle with Eh K'Nyaw, heading up to a hard-to-reach, secluded village, I felt an internal tug-of-war: happy for Maria and her newfound ministry, but dreadfully aware of my inadequacy in caring for the villagers who now filled our humble porch daily with medical needs.

I prayed, "Lord Jesus, what shall I do?"

The thought entering my mind surprised me: *Train the students!*

Actually, that solution had been part of our initial vision—to train the young to become medics and medical missionaries, combining natural remedies with medical skills while sharing Jesus' love in service.

But how, Lord?

Oddly, His answer came in the form of a theft. When Maria visited our home, her tool for transportation, a motorcycle, was stolen from right under our porch. This left her stranded at our place where she was able to observe my conundrum firsthand. It became clear to any observer that even if Paul or I were gifted and trained with more advanced medical skills, because of two toddlers and several more small children now living in our home—and our homeschooling Anna and Josiah—there weren't enough leftover hours to help our porch patients adequately.

Three times that motorcycle was stolen from Maria, and three times Paul and Eh K'Nyaw were able to find where it was hidden and to bring it back! Not only did that extra time with us enable my daughter to observe fully our predicament, but also that realization inspired her with the idea to teach medical skills to a team of students. Then, whenever they had free time from their studies, those young people could assist me on the porch. Maria even made up a curriculum for them.

Soon a team of nine excited students met daily with our daughter on the porch, soaking up all the knowledge she could impart. They were the perfect answer to our dilemma, because now there was no longer a need for a translator. The students could communicate *directly* with the sick regarding their health issues.

Meanwhile, during this training process, Maria faithfully rode back and forth from her mountain home to train the students. And while in the mountains, she became skilled in many different ways. After all, she was the only medical person available, and it was often too far to travel to a hospital in time for a patient's survival.

Maria was 18 years old by then, and she loved mountain life. Villagers had given her a simple wooden hut, where she set up a space for her home with another space partitioned off for her clinic.

Meanwhile, she made friends with her neighbors, including many of the village children. During evenings she would go visiting, stooping down to enter neighboring bamboo huts, adjusting her eyes to the dark and to the smoke coming from the fire in the middle of the dwelling.

One time, as she sat with a family around their fire while her eyes adjusted to the room, she noticed a pile of something resembling rats stacked beside her. She watched as the people speared the rats and roasted them over the fire.

Breaking off a crunchy tail, a woman offered it to her. "It's really good, Tharamo!"

Maria politely declined.

One dark night she awoke with a start when she heard men calling, "Tharamo! Come, Tharamo! A man is injured!"

With her medical bag in one hand and a flashlight in the other, Maria followed the group to another village hut. Apparently, a drunk man had been involved in a fight and was hit in the head with a machete, causing a sizable gash.

Evaluating the situation, she decided to set up a treatment table right there. After praying, Maria then asked someone to aim the flashlight at the gash. Another couple of people held the drunk man down as she injected lidocaine, cleaned the wound, and stitched it up. She left her patient with antibiotics, then returned every day to change his dressing. To her delight, he healed nicely without infection.

My daughter chuckled to herself when she noticed some of the villagers nodding to one another and asking, "Does not a great doctor now live among us?"

CHAPTER 19

Emily

Having finished her teaching commitment in the Thai Karen mountain school, Emily had returned home. About that time, Dan turned up again, asking if Emily would be willing to go and teach among the mountain people in Karen State. He ended his invitation by saying she was really needed there.

Born loving adventure, Emily thought the challenging trek into such a remote and primitive place would be exciting. She was known for her long strides and—for a girl—unusual endurance and strength. Emily would call me biased for describing her as a hidden gem with a servant's heart, a peacemaker who would take the blame rather than letting it go to someone else. But I've seen that scenario played out in her life since she was a child. This opportunity for Emily to live in the mountains of Karen State was an answer to her heart's call; her dream would finally be fulfilled if God allowed her to serve there.

What follows is an excerpt from her own writings after she had experienced mountain life in Karen State for a while: *I have been teaching in the mountains of "No Man's Land." It takes several days of strenuous hiking to get in or out. I arrived "out" this week to renew my Thai visa. It's the rainy season, so the trail is mud soup, and there were leeches. I got so dirty, it seemed like my skin would be stained permanently. But I had plenty of energy, and it was great!*

In May, on the spur of a moment, a friend invited me to go to this remote place in Karen State and teach. I was scared, but still agreed to it. A few days later we started the trek together with a group of Karen.

I had a vague expectation of foggy scenes. But on the second day of the trip, a surprising perception stole over me as I was sitting against a tree. The meadow and mountains were very beautiful, indeed, but I felt something else, something different from anything I'd felt before—a pervasive peace.

The rice fields surprised me next. Up until that time, to me a rice field was, well, a rice field. But I'd never walked through one, especially not one like this. They fill every valley, and they patch the mountains with green. Not just any green, but an absolutely glowing green. As we hiked, their simple beauty thrilled my heart until I was too tired to enjoy anything anymore. (Later, I got to get in the mud myself and learn to plant rice, standing knee-deep in water.) Tending rice fields from seed to harvest is no easy task. The people have to work really hard. Whatever they want to eat, they have to grow. Wherever they want to travel, they have to walk. But it's like you enter another land, a place where the people all carry their burdens together and enjoy one another. Whether working in the fields or roasting corn in the fireplace, they artlessly share life, work, and pleasure. Although I realize these people are not perfect, their unity was universal enough that I couldn't miss it.

I got to live much like those mountain people do. (My friend was the only other pale face I'd see for two months at a time.) They fed me as much rice and jungle vegetables as I could eat. And my mom told me later that I looked really healthy. Everything is cooked over fire. At a Karen meal, there is a circle of plates heaped high with rice. In the middle are bowls of vegetable broth, steamed vegetables, fish paste, and sometimes curry or pounded chili dip. We sit cross-legged around the food and mix small spoonful of the dishes into our rice with our fingers, sipping vegetable broth from a common spoon. The host urges everyone to take more rice.

I had to learn how to bathe in a river while I wore a sarong. Thankfully, my skills have improved since I first came, and no one has reason to feel sorry for me anymore. We wash all our laundry on the rocks at the river.

The school is a big one-room bamboo-and-wood building. There are ten grades and ten teachers, too. Education is taken very seriously and as professionally as possible. There are no desks or chairs, nothing except pinewood blackboards that must be blackened every week. Everyone attends school in bare feet, including the teachers. Sandals are left at the entrance. Students have few, if any, textbooks. They must copy their lessons. The classrooms are divided by blue curtains, and are open at the front. This gives the teachers an opportunity to gain valuable insights from other classes as the children copy their lessons. No cruel or unusual measures of punishment are inflicted. Students who don't meet their teacher's expectations must cross their arms, grab their ears, and do a series of up and down squats, even if they are teenagers. If the teacher is in the mood, he or she can further vary this by sending her naughty students to perform before specified classrooms . . .

I slept in the girls' dorm, a bamboo house. The girls came with a delightful variety of personalities. Two of my roommates made the most of every opportunity to laugh at me. I loved it! For example, when I was startled by a chicken and overreacted, my roommates lay on their backs chuckling loudly. Or when I tried to share how huge a spider (really) was when it ambled past my sleeping mat, I didn't get much sympathy.

One thing that stands out about those mountain people is that they are very industrious. Another is that they are deeply devoted to God. They get up around 4 a.m. to start fires. At 5 o'clock the students gather to sing, pray, and study the Bible. They end the day that way, too. When not in school, everyone keeps busy. There are fires to build, rice to cook, clothes to wash, vegetables to search for, gardens to hoe, rice fields to tend—endless work to do.

Sometime after Emily arrived at her mountain post deep in Karen State, she was told of a 17-year-old man who had stepped on a land mine. He was in critical condition at the local clinic, a half-hour's walk away. It was not known if he would survive, but the medics at the small, primitive clinic would try to keep him alive until they could transport him to a hospital in Thailand. He faced a 16-hour trek with friends carrying him on a crude bamboo stretcher through rice fields, jungles, and over steep mountains.

Before they could begin the trip, however, the medics realized the young man would not survive the journey unless they found someone to donate blood, because the patient had already bled too much. Of even more concern was finding a match to his rare blood type. Although people far and near were tested, no one's blood type matched the patient's.

At last, in desperation, knowing without a blood transfusion this young man had no chance of survival, the medics decided to ask Emily. She had no clue about her blood type, but was more than willing to donate some of her blood—if it worked. Amazingly, the God who cares for the sparrow that falls, had placed Emily with the right blood type at the right place at the right time!

Although the medics couldn't test Emily's blood for any diseases, they were able to transfuse their patient. And the young man, with some of my daughter's blood flowing through his veins, survived the long, painful trek to a medical center. Sadly, he lost his leg, but today he is well and strong with a beautiful wife and child.

Meanwhile, the Burmese army was moving ever closer to their area. But Emily needed to renew her Thai visa, and that necessity opened the opportunity for her to leave immediately, bringing her time in the mountains of Karen State to an abrupt end.

Assisted by trustworthy Karen National Union (KNU) soldiers, she was able to make the gruesome, three-day trek out. They were also able to slip through the forested mountains, allowing Emily to return safely to Thailand without any trouble from the Burmese. And before long, her visa was renewed and she was back at the family home near the lime orchard.

Uncertain what God's will was for her now, Emily wished it could be the mountains in Karen State again. But how was she to be equipped to serve, because she didn't really feel called to be a teacher? So she decided to wait on God's leading, meanwhile retreating to the same Karen mountain village in Thailand where her sister Maria had previously lived.

At first, Emily shared a hut with two other women. Later, she lived in an abandoned Catholic church in that same village. She was the only Seventh-day Adventist there, but she loved her time in those mountains, the long hikes, and the immersion with the people and their culture—true fulfillment!

Being young and adventuresome, Emily would sometimes hike the one-hour distance from the road back up the mountain to the village in the dark by herself. One evening as she jumped off the truck she had taken up the mountain to the mouth of the trail leading to her village, she decided not to search for her flashlight. Instead, she would enjoy a true night-walk as she used to experience with her sister Maria and their friend Noah during their childhood. The difference was that this footpath was winding and narrow, and there were snakes—poisonous ones, too. Undaunted by the possible dangers, Emily actually reveled in groping her way through the brush in the dark. At last, without incident, she reached the church where she lived.

The next morning she was the talk of the village. Her superstitious neighbors were astounded that she wasn't afraid of the evil spirits as she had maneuvered through the night without even a flashlight.

Next, God made a way for Emily to attend AFCOE, the Amazing Facts College of Evangelism in California. He even provided funds for her admission and for transportation to take her to the campus where she learned how to reach people for Jesus.

Returning to the Karen people, Emily was happy, indeed. But the next few years held unexpected health challenges for her. At times, though, she was well enough to return to her beloved Karen mountains, then work with Gayle Haberkam.

After several bouts with malaria and dengue fever, Emily seemed to have suffered a reaction to one of the drugs used to treat the diseases while she was at a hospital. Then, when living in a remote area again, she became frightened when she noticed strange sensations of heaviness in her limbs, along with numbness and tingling, and her tongue kept rolling back into her throat.

"Lord," she prayed, "what's wrong with me? I can hardly walk."

Emily decided it was time to visit Gayle down the mountain. But what normally took only an hour stretched out much longer, and she barely made it to the Haberkam home. Gayle immediately brought our daughter the rest of the way to our house. Because we thought Emily must be fighting some common illness, Paul and I suggested she go to bed. But when she didn't appear the next morning, I became alarmed.

"Emily, what's wrong? Why are you still in bed?"

"I don't know, Mama. I can't get myself up. My arms and legs are numb, and my heart is beating a mile a minute. I think I'm about to die!"

It would take our daughter several years to gain back her health. Her symptoms started to subside after she was diagnosed and treated for severe Vitamin B-12 deficiency.

As Emily regained her health, we've been deeply touched by how she has given of herself to our large extended family. Over the last few years, she has faithfully and selflessly served in our home, helping both Paul and me, but also caring for her increasing number of "sisters and brothers" in our house; that care included cooking, cleaning, and even watching over children when they were sick. Emily has also helped with her brother Josiah's homeschooling. Moreover, our daughter goes about her work quietly in the background, often unnoticed.

Our dear friend Gayle once compared Emily and her humble attributes to an orchid. The analogy was perfect for Thailand, where well over a thousand different species of orchids thrive in the country's thick forests. Not surprisingly, the orchid has earned its rightful place as Thailand's national floral symbol.

Here are Gayle's own words: "Emily is an orchid of rarest bloom, opening to its fullest beauty in the midst of a deep jungle where nobody is present to appreciate it."

CHAPTER 20

Surprises

During our first year on the mission field, we managed to provide for Sunshine Orchard through Paul's parents helping us financially. Support also came from our Montana church and from other friends. Later, though, we learned that Paul's family business was not doing well, so his parents could no longer continue their support as before.

Despite our decision to live by faith, we were still concerned and, thus, sent prayers heavenward. Meanwhile, the Thailand director of Adventist Development and Relief Agency (ADRA) phoned us, asking if he could bring an elderly Japanese gentleman to visit. Within an hour, Mr. Kakimoto arrived with his daughter and board members from a charitable organization in Singapore.

After asking some simple questions about us, the Karen children, the history of the school, and about our medical outreach, the board members also inquired about how we financed it all. We shared that ours was a faith-based ministry, so we didn't solicit funds for or advertise about Sunshine Orchard (our convictions at that time). When asked to see our budget, we admitted to not having one. But when we faced a much-needed project, we prayed and God provided the funds.

I couldn't help thinking that God also provided some very talented teenaged boys at our school, boys gifted in bamboo construction. They even used wet bamboo strips to hold everything together. When those strips dried, they formed a tight bond, creating sturdy floors, walls, bannisters, railings, and stairs.

Although those young men had replaced the temporary shabby boys' and girls' dorms with more substantial bamboo structures, I still cringed when the board members asked to see our Sunshine Orchard campus. There were so many more improvements needed.

As we all strolled around the school grounds, showing those gracious people the bamboo buildings, Paul and I found ourselves apologizing for how primitive everything looked.

Their response surprised us: "It's amazing!"

We soon felt God's presence as we continued to tour the property with our visitors. At the same time, our hearts were touched by their genuine interest in the children and our work. Paul and I felt as if we were walking on holy ground while God seemed to give us all a gift of mutual respect for one another.

Because of this impromptu meeting and tour, our mission was blessed with funds for the initial permanent construction projects, for food, salaries, and the supplies needed on a monthly basis to cover 120 students and staff—and even for our medical relief work!

To describe Paul and me as flabbergasted wouldn't be accurate enough. We were bowled over with awe at how God had used a Buddhist, Baptist, and Pentecostal team all the way from Singapore to bless every one of Sunshine Orchard's children. At the same time, we felt God's approval that we were exactly where He wanted us to be.

I also admit to a new sense of relaxation, because this immense gift would banish our monthly stress over collecting enough funds to feed and care for all our students. Even the salaries for our school's staff would be provided! I shouldn't have relaxed so much, though, because Paul and I were about to receive another surprise.

We were enjoying a lengthy trip to Chiang Mai to buy goods for the school. After 24 hours in that city, Old Trusty Rusty was packed full with needed supplies when we headed back.

Returning to Sunshine Orchard, we suddenly faced a huge

number of ragtag youngsters with torn clothing, matted hair, and dirty bare feet.

Who are all these children?

Eh K'Nyaw quickly arrived on the scene and confirmed our fears. The youngsters had all come out of the conflict area over the border in Karen State where fighting had resumed. And each child needed a safe place to take shelter.

"Tharamo," Eh K'Nyaw said, "there are 140 new children!"

I smiled, because I knew exactly what my husband was thinking: the words of Jesus from Mark10:14: *"". . . Let the little children come to Me, and do not forbid them; for of such is the kingdom of God"* (NKJV).

And that was how our boarding students increased to 260 in number.

Evidently, God wanted us to remain on our tiptoes and not become too comfortable. We realized then that all our dependency should rest totally on Him and not on a secure income to provide for our now-growing needs. Yes, we often lacked funds for everything but bare necessities. But it was an amazing walk of faith as all genuine needs were supplied.

From the very dawn of our ministry in Thailand, we decided to extend to our neighbors all the good we possibly could. And we considered our neighbor to be anyone coming to our door or asking for help; it also meant venturing into surrounding villages and making ourselves available. Then we would use our time and talents, trusting God to provide and enable us to pay our neighbors' hospital bills—even for expensive surgeries, medicines, and food to feed the hungry. Admittedly, many times the ATM machine would show an almost-empty account while large sums were due for patients' bills. And then I'd revert to my old self when anxiety twisted my stomach, and I'd try to figure out a solution on my own. Standing there helpless, I'd again realize that only God had the solution. So to Him we would go with our request. Then to our great joy, the funds so desperately needed would appear in our account (for some reason, usually at the very last moment).

One such experience occurred after being handed a hospital bill for one of the patients we had intended to transport back to his village. But the patient would not be released unless his bill was paid first. I knew there wasn't much money left in our account. And sure enough, no miracle awaited me at the ATM machine. Returning to our vehicle where Paul was resting, I told him the situation, then asked, "What shall we do?"

My husband was his usually calm self while I fretted, trying to come up with a solution. At last, after exhausting all our possibilities, we decided to pray. (That should have been our initial action, but even missionaries are human and fail at times to call upon God *first*.)

Paul and I knelt in the truck and asked the Lord to make a way to provide for the hospital bill. I then returned to the ATM, checking the balance again. This time I found plenty of funds for the hospital bill—and even for other needs!

We never learned how the Lord provided that time or whom He had used. The fact remains, however, God is the same today as in biblical times when He placed tax money in a fish. God has never let us down. We weren't always able to purchase everything we desired for the school or to build the exact buildings we wanted. But He provided—little by little and time after time—and the work moved forward, not backward.

Our behavior might be considered presumptuous or, at least, teetering on the verge of presumption. But from the very start, everything about our calling to the mission field to the birthing of Sunshine Orchard was through dependency upon God to provide the money to support our mission.

There was one area, however, in which we slowly changed our minds, that of fundraising. Through the counsel of people from our own denomination as well as those from other walks of faith, we learned about presenting our mission's needs before others. We were told that not to do so would rob others of "partnering" with our work. Many people do want to donate to worthy causes, they said, but donors need information about the ministries first. With those ideas new to us, it was with some hesitancy we gave our consent for good friends to make a list for our presentations while on furlough. From then on, we shared about our ministry whenever we were invited to present a slide program at various churches in the USA.

Although I suffered from mixed feelings about sharing in regards to our ministry, I realized we now had 140 extra children at Sunshine Orchard—children who were in tremendous need. Therefore, I soon learned to prepare a newsletter and other communications to broadcast this news and other issues pertaining to our mission school. Although we began to see resulting funds come in that way, God still surprised us with monetary gifts from totally unexpected donors!

CHAPTER 21

The River Property

Rumors seemed to abound more often after the latest young refugees arrived on our side of the border—not of another 140 children, but of over a thousand, slowly making their way through the jungle toward Sunshine Orchard! Paul, Anna, Josiah, and I were in the United States at that time for our then-yearly visa run when we heard that these desperate children were soon to arrive at our mission. My husband simply quoted Mark 10:14 again. Then after prayer, the two of us committed the possible predicament to God.

I kept thinking of the river property across the road from Sunshine Orchard as the solution to the new numbers of children recently arrived plus any more who might join them in the future—if, indeed, the rumors materialized. But I kept those thoughts to myself.

One Sabbath afternoon we were relaxing at the home of longtime friends, Lauren and Donna Staffords; their parents, former missionaries, were there, also. When they asked questions about the current situation in Thailand, we shared all the news, including the rumors of more children possibly on their way. Then I blurted out that my husband didn't know, but I felt impressed about something and hadn't shared it with him yet.

Before I could finish, Paul said in his matter-of-fact way, "God wants us to purchase the river property."

Astonished, I asked, "How did you know what I've been thinking?"

He then admitted that those same thoughts had been invading his mind as well.

Despite the property's expensive cost and the fact that we had no funds at all saved for such a purchase, not even for a down payment, our friends encouraged us to "step out in faith."

We spent the next few weeks in the United States on the road, sharing in churches about Sunshine Orchard. As a result, we received around $10,000 in donations for our ministry. Because of that amazing amount, we decided to proceed in faith regarding the river property and, at the same time, doing our part in the fund-raising effort.

When we phoned Gayle Haberkam, we asked if she was willing to talk with the owner of the river property. Gayle agreed to the visit and subsequently arranged for us to pay a down payment of $17,000 within a couple of days. We knew from experience and from God's precious promises that everything is possible with Him. But I decided He needed my help in raising the remaining $7,000. So I crossed the Canadian border to visit a friend who owned a printing business. She agreed to help me put together some newsletters that I could mail to supporters.

On my way back from my friend's place that night, driving the winding country road, I suddenly realized that even if those newsletters were mailed the next day, people wouldn't receive them in time to respond before the deadline date for the down payment. (Those were the days before we had acquired enough email addresses to use for such fund-raising campaigns. So we needed to rely on mailing the letters the old-fashioned way.)

I sighed, telling the Lord that, apparently, my efforts had been a waste of time. So now it was up to Him to bring in the $7,000—if

He wanted us to purchase the river property to extend the Sunshine Orchard campus for our newcomers.

I felt oddly subdued as I continued to commune with Him. Moreover, the drive was awe-inspiring as stars sparkled in the dark skies above. I also reminded myself that God had a thousand ways to provide for His work if He wanted it to go forward.

As I entered the home on a lonely mountain where we were staying during part of our furlough, Paul was talking on the phone. Listening to his part of the conversation triggered my curiosity. At last he put down the phone, then calmly announced that we had all the funds needed for the down payment. God had provided without our newsletters—and without anyone knowing yet about the property!

The call came from the daughter of some missionaries stationed in Chiang Mai. Living in Canada with her family, this generous child of God had felt impressed to send $7,000—and it was already in the mail! (How can we ever doubt that God is actively involved in the lives of those who serve Him?) So now we were able to pay a down payment on that beautiful river property. Another amazing journey in faith had begun.

A miracle then occurred at a church about this time. Paul had just finished his slide program regarding Sunshine Orchard and was packing up to leave when a man approached him. The latecomer had missed most of Paul's presentation. But he was curious and wanted to know more. So my husband stayed and enjoyed telling the gentleman all about our mission. When returning to Thailand, we received word from that same man that he was sending $5,000. We were immensely grateful.

But that wasn't the end of this donor's contributions. When another large payment was due, he wrote us, asking how much more was needed. He then sent another substantial amount. In all, throughout the years, this gentleman and his wife have donated many thousands to Sunshine Orchard.

Considering how the relationship began with just a meeting

between two men who love God, we never dreamed how that meeting would develop into a beautiful relationship between our families over time. I admit we feared they would think we treasure them only because of their generosity. And of course, we're grateful. But even if they had never given anything to our mission, they would mean just as much to us. And let me assure you, Paul never asked them for a dime. It was God who did all the asking!

After our furlough, we returned to our beloved Karen people and the school that God had placed in our hands. We quickly arranged to meet with the river property's owner to make further arrangements for the purchase. Because we couldn't communicate in Thai, we asked a friend to be our mediator and translator in the matter. She explained the terms: we would make payments over a year's time. In addition to the down payment, which was already paid, we owed half of the remainder in six months and the final amount at the end of the year. We were able to make that commitment, because we had already seen how God provided the down payment.

The owner, however, didn't stick to her part of the arrangement. Instead, she would contact us frequently through our Thai friend, telling us that an early payment needed to be deposited into her bank account. She claimed that creditors were knocking on her door and might take the land. Amazingly, each time that happened, God provided us with the $6,000 she usually demanded—when we never had extra funds just sitting in the bank!

Equally important, we still had to trust God to provide for the next sick villager's medical bill or for food to feed all the added children. (Instead of a thousand new arrivals from Burma, as rumored, however, the number was under fifty, increasing our students to a total of about 300.)

Each time the property owner phoned for an early payment, the request turned into a miracle. Almost all those funds came from no more than a handful of believers who were impressed to contribute.

I recall one such time when $30,000 was needed the next day, and I told Paul I just had to get away to a quiet place and pray. I felt overwhelmed by the heavy burden of such a huge amount as I knelt by the guesthouse bed during the day and evening.

Taking a break and booting up our computer, I noticed a new email. It read, "We were just looking at your website . . . and still appreciate all you and your family did for us years ago. How can we send you $30,000?" I was stunned and burst into tears. God had done it again through generous Christians!

As the time drew nearer for our final payment on the river property, I noticed unusual activity on that land across the road. A fellowship meal get-together was my first guess. But almost immediately, I realized it was no picnic for people. It was a spirit ceremony with laden tables of food and opened bottles of soft drinks. More and more was brought out until the large tabletops were full.

"What a waste!" I thought. Were they doing this for the final sale of the property? If they were, then would their "spirits" get the credit instead of God? That possibility bothered me.

But soon the real story emerged, and the truth was humbling. The "sacrifice" of food was to encourage the spirits to *leave* the property and for them to find a home elsewhere. The woman who owned that land, apparently *in faith*, already figured the property to be sold. And we, as new owners, have our own God. Thus, the spirits had to go!

This woman, a Buddhist and animist, in a way was displaying enormous faith in the existence of *our* God! She had already removed the huge reclining golden Buddha from the Buddhist meditation center (which we hoped to be a future Christian medical training and treatment facility). She had removed the pigs from the property a couple of weeks before. And now she was asking the spirits to go while she provided for their journey.

I had heard she told a group that we were "good, good people." She had pointed to my husband Paul and said that he "drives and drives" to the hospital with the sick, "not eating or sleeping." She, a

Thai, had declared that our Karen students and younger children are also trained to be "good." Paul and I lowered our heads when we heard this, because we were not solely responsible for this work; God was. God was also using our staff and volunteers, and we were all simply instruments in His hands.

The day finally arrived when the river property was paid in full. Now that land along the lovely meandering Moei River belonged to our ministry because of two very generous donors along with many others whose smaller donations added up to the entire purchase price.

CHAPTER 22

Maria's Love Story

Unknown to me, Maria had been suffering in silence for quite some time. As a very private person, she didn't share with us much about her inward struggles. Moreover, she didn't want to cause us any stress or be a negative influence on her younger siblings. Inwardly, though, she was questioning everything she had been taught, including the very existence of a loving God. After all, how could a loving God allow her precious father, Eddie, to be taken from his children who had needed him so much?

Furthermore, when the call came to the mission field, Maria reluctantly decided to go along, but was rebelling inside. It didn't take much time, though, for the needy Karen people—especially the children—to steal her heart. Then she became a willing captive in foreign mission service for life.

Maria wasn't interested in getting married. But Luke 1:37 assures us that God is the provider of impossibilities, and apparently, He already had a good "impossibility" for our daughter. Before He brought a young man named Jordan into Maria's life, however, God healed her emotionally and spiritually. Part of that healing God brought about by putting an abandoned baby into Maria's care when she was seventeen years old.

Maria and Jordan had corresponded for a few years on and off because of a mutual interest in emergency medical services (EMS). She had first noticed Jordan on a Young Disciples web page, and she was impressed with his comments. Because she remained anonymous, he wasn't aware of her presence there. Later, while on another online site, Maria was quite surprised at receiving a friendship request from Jordan. At that time, their communication focused only on EMS issues and missions.

Once in a while, we would tease Maria about Jordan, and she would stoutly declare that he was shorter than she and, of course, he would never be interested in her.

One day I received a call from Jordan about coming as a volunteer to Sunshine Orchard Learning Center. I had already heard good things about him, so I told him he was welcome; but as events played out, he couldn't come our way that year. Instead, he served the Lord (and people) in Afghanistan. The following year Maria informed us that Jordan was, indeed, coming to Sunshine Orchard, because he was intrigued by the work we were doing and thought it would be a good experience for him.

Sometime before this, Maria had met Jordan in person while on a visa-renewal furlough and a visit with relatives in the United States. Caught on the spur of the moment, Maria had ventured outside, barefoot, to meet Jordan in the snow while he and his siblings piled out of a car to greet her. She admitted later to being somewhat surprised that he was not shorter than she, but actually, quite a bit taller. And Jordan later revealed he thought she must be a little crazy because of going without shoes or boots in the snow!

Their next meeting was at the airport in Bangkok. Soon thereafter, Maria and Jordan ended up serving together, conducting medical work in the Thai mountains above Sunshine Orchard. (During that time, they fell in love—but never revealed their true feelings for each other.)

Every now and then while in Thailand, Jordan was able to use his medical expertise to help our ministry. At one such time, I had become quite impatient. It was one of those frustrating days when we just couldn't seem to get out of the house, as planned. Unending interruptions kept our family, including Jordan, from heading to Old Trusty Rusty for our trip to the city.

To our surprise, into our home stumbled a weary father from across the river, carrying a boy on his back. Then the man carefully unloaded the child onto our floor. Jordan and Maria quickly evaluated him. I heard words such as "pneumonia" and "intestinal blockage," and, immediately, we all headed to the truck with the patient and his father. Next, Old Trusty Rusty's motor roared to life, then began its journey toward a hospital in Mae Sot.

Our young passenger was admitted, and we received word that, yes, he did have an intestinal blockage and a severe case of pneumonia, both of which were being treated. But the doctors found something else wrong, something involving the boy's heart.

Upon hearing that Mae Sot didn't have the equipment to diagnose the heart problem, we took the child many more miles, all the way to a hospital in Chiang Mai. There they discovered three large holes in the boy's heart!

At eight years old, living in a war-torn jungle village without health care, the youngster had been viewed as simply "weak"—and spent most of his life watching others his age roam fields, work in gardens, and play soccer and other games. But this child had no energy to join in.

Now God blessed, and we were able to arrange for the boy to undergo surgery. In fact, that year, he was in and out of the hospital for several surgeries; and finally, the boy was sent home with the ability to attend school, to play, and to join friends in roaming the fields and mountains.

God's timing was perfect. He cared so much for a little jungle boy that He must have sent angels to hinder our departure again and again, so that child could receive the heart surgeries he needed to revolutionize his life.

Jordan finally returned to the United States. But the young man phoned Paul and me soon thereafter to ask for permission to continue communication with our daughter on a "deeper level." That's how Maria discovered that their feelings were mutual. A long-distance courtship then took place over the next two years while Jordan finished nursing school.

5

The Planting of the Lord

CHAPTER 23

Calling of the Steck Family

Paul and I worked together with the school's staff, all of us making most day-to-day decisions together as a team. The school had been without an actual principal for quite some time, because the former principal had taken a different job. Admittedly, we needed a principal, but were not willing to hire just anyone. We wanted someone who shared the vision God had placed on our hearts for these special children.

Because we couldn't find a Karen educator to lead the academic part of the school and to help us reorganize and boost its quality to higher standards, we were urged to find a "foreigner" to fill the position. (Most qualified Karen were either already in demand from other schools or had emigrated to another country.)

With the school's problem still unsolved, our furlough arrived, and we found ourselves on a very busy speaking tour in the U.S. Although without much time to relax, we treasured those moments with God's family. Our friends, the Staffords, joined us, and traveling together was such a blessing.

While on the road, arriving at the Northport, Washington, Seventh-day Adventist Church, we were invited by the Steck family to stay at their home. Brenda Steck had spent some time in Thailand during her youth, and she was excited about our visit. She even served us Thai food! (Meanwhile, someone had mentioned to us that Brenda had shared her dream of returning someday to Thailand as a missionary. But her husband Harvey hadn't shown much interest in mission service.)

As guests in the Stecks' home, we were glad for the opportunity to get to know them better. And before long, we asked Harvey to consider joining us at Sunshine Orchard Learning Center as our school's new principal. At first, he seemed uninterested. Then after hearing details about our mission school, to our amazement, Harvey was soon talking about the school as *his* school! Brenda looked surprised by her husband's interest as well.

The primitive and unorganized environment at Sunshine Orchard did not seem a great threat to Brenda, because she had already lived in that kind of environment as a "missionary kid." So we asked Harvey if he wanted to visit Sunshine Orchard and stay for a month. That way, he could assess the place in person. (Also, we had enough money at that time to cover his travel expenses.) We expected Harvey to love the school, although it was a rough jewel in the Master's hand.

When he arrived at our mission, Harvey saw at once the need for more organization and how much his and his family's skills could offer. He also perceived how God had begun a beautiful work and had already instilled in many of the students a deep desire to labor for the Lord.

After Harvey returned home, he took the lead and started to raise funds, asking God to provide a specific amount—*if this was truly His will.* God did provide the funds, and in July of 2011, the Steck family—Harvey, Brenda, their daughters Sharon, age 19, and Hannah, age 16—arrived at Sunshine Orchard. In fact, their arrival started a housing "chain reaction" of sorts.

As mentioned, all three of our daughters had mixed feelings about our wooden house with glass in the windows, feelings hovering between disgust and embarrassment. Their attitude grew out of a perception of how our living conditions differed from those surrounding us. They asked if we could all move over to the school and live in a bamboo hut. That desire wouldn't become a reality until the Stecks arrived. In fact, the rainy season—in full force—quickly advanced the decision that the Stecks move into our house. While our furlough lasted a little longer, we ordered a simple-but-spacious-enough bamboo house built to accommodate our growing family.

Our "hut" was erected right in the middle of the bustling campus in the lime orchard. The skilled older students and some of the staff built our home in a week's time. The new abode was rustic, but I loved the way light filtered through the bamboo walls. Otherwise, everything inside would have been dark. I also loved listening to the night sounds through the open windows. The house had a natural "warmth" about it.

Although initially, our new place was enthralling (and I've continued to love bamboo huts), the newness of ours wore off quickly. The house brought greater challenges with sanitation. The villagers' scant knowledge about such unseen things as germs provided them with a certain bliss, which I found myself envying during my anxiety and helplessness over such issues.

At the same time, there was a silent disapproval of our germ awareness. Why use soap? Why worry about dirty water? And why be so alarmed about a little blood smeared wherever a good place was found to wipe it off? And why do you need a napkin or tissue when there is such a handy thing as a shirt? No need for diapers when you have a skirt to wipe with. Having cracks in the floor is a perfect place to spit, vomit, or for the baby to use as a toilet. And then just smear it down the cracks in the floor with your fingers!

We had visitors who didn't seem to understand that we were, indeed, trying to do our best. It was suggested that we keep a bucket of Clorox water at the entrance for people to wash their feet and hands before they entered. This was an excellent idea for those who had only a few visitors at a time—and a door! Our entrance was a 10-foot-wide opening in the wall, welcoming anyone—student, staff member, neighbor, or villager—to come on in. As a custom, everyone would remove his or her shoes before entering. It was not so much the dirt from the outside that concerned us, but the unsanitary habits, which were ingrained, as noted earlier.

It was during the rainy season that we fought with sickness the most. Rotavirus came to stay for a while, infecting all of the little ones. This terrible illness could cause severe diarrhea and eventual death if not treated as quickly as possible. (We sometimes even had babies hooked up to IVs.) Again, we saw how very fragile life could be in this kind of environment.

June and July were fly season in those parts, and it made me go on a frantic campaign, trying to cleanse at least our living space from the pests. But that was really hard with the ten-foot-wide entrance into our home!

The best part of our bamboo hut was the tiled floor in our kitchen, something unheard of in our area. To my delight, that unique floor kept our kitchen more sanitary for meal preparation.

And all that while, Harvey Steck was doing his best to organize the school. (We will be forever grateful to the Steck family for their years of service at Sunshine Orchard.)

CHAPTER 24

A Gentle Giant and a Thief

At another time Anna, Emily, Eh K'Nyaw, and I were blessed when God turned a two-hour delay into a divine appointment. We had spent the morning in dealing with a difficult situation, which had taken two hours longer far from home than we had planned.

During our drive back, our youngest daughter Anna informed us she needed to check on patients at a hospital. When we dropped her off at its entrance, Eh K'Nyaw saw some of "our patients" by the road. The woman had been discharged much earlier than expected, and we praised the Lord that we would be able to take her and her husband home to their village.

She climbed into our truck and sat between Eh K'Nyaw and Emily. When Anna returned, she sat in the front seat while the patient's husband climbed up into the cargo bed. With Eh K'Nyaw interpreting, I soon realized that our passenger knew him and our Anna. Giggling, the Karen woman told us that many of her fellow patients thought that Anna was her daughter. Each time Anna had visited, the girl had brought food for her. And those watching were convinced that only a daughter would be so attentive. What amused the woman even more was that they thought she had a *white* Karen daughter!

I became quite curious about this woman who was a patient

among many, so decided to start quizzing her through Eh K'Nyaw's excellent interpretive skills. (Admittedly, I was often told that I asked too many questions. The villagers didn't tell me this—just my "culturally correct" children.) But I charged ahead, asking such questions as, what was her health issue? Did she receive treatment? Is she better? Could she describe her symptoms? What did they do for her in the hospital? What medication did they give her? And what was she going to do now?

"I will go to the witch doctor," she replied, "because they were unable to make me completely well at the hospital."

"What will the witch doctor do for you?" Upon her reply, I looked into the rearview mirror and asked Eh K'Nyaw, "Please tell her that the God in Heaven is stronger than the witch doctor. Tell her that He is a personal God and that He is her Friend." Then I added, "Tell her that He has promised, if she seeks Him, she will find Him."

After listening intently to Eh K'Nyaw, this mountain woman then surprised us by sharing that she had attended a Christian school when she was a little girl, and she also used to pray when she was a child. Moreover, she could read and write—quite unusual for those parts. In fact, when the hospital staff admitted patients from the mountain villages, the staff didn't expect them to know how to write. Therefore, they brought an inkpad for a thumbprint instead of asking for a signature.

The woman revealed further that her husband had taught himself how to read. That was unheard of. She next told us that now she worshipped the spirits, but her children attended our school in their remote mountain village where four of our Sunshine Orchard students taught during their school break. She admitted that she felt too timid to join the singing and praying at the school with her children in the mornings, but she loved to listen to them.

Then I asked her if she would do something for me. Would she read the Bible if I gave her one?

"Yes, of course!" she exclaimed in the Karen language.

And would she talk to God as a friend about everything (her sickness, her fears, etc.)?

Again, she replied in the affirmative.

Much more was discussed, and I believe with my whole heart that this was, indeed, another divine appointment. When I asked if her husband would mind reading the things we gave her, I smiled when she described him as a *lizard*.

Then she explained, "He *snatches* any books or papers I come home with, so he will be happy!"

Old Trusty Rusty delivered the couple to their village with the woman carrying a Bible and the book, *Steps to Christ*, both printed in their language. As I watched them disappear among the huts, I prayed that God's perfect will would continue to be done in their lives.

Upon returning home, we heard a rumor swirling around campus. A dangerous thief was in the area, stealing from the staff houses at night. Many were filled with fear, wondering who would be the thief's next victim.

Paul awakened in the middle of the night when someone came to our entrance, telling him the thief was on the prowl again. After our prayer together, my husband decided to head out to see what the dreaded thief was up to this time.

With everything in the orchard seeming quiet, Paul decided to check on Principal Steck's house. Because of a full moon, there was no need for a flashlight. And with the stars twinkling brightly in the night sky, Paul actually enjoyed the stillness (which was so different from daytime when exuberant children often scampered around all over the property).

As my husband continued to hike, he could detect the form of a man coming toward him. Assuming the fellow must be the thief, Paul calmly approached the man, taking him firmly by the arm and removing a large bag hanging from the culprit's shoulder. Paul then opened the bag to search its contents. First, he spotted a dangerous-looking knife, but the remaining items all seemed to be edibles, obviously from the Stecks' house. My husband then realized the man was simply hungry.

Next, Paul lifted a container of noodles from the bag, but left a loaf of bread, some fruit, and other food for the thief. All the while, the man did nothing, just stood there as if paralyzed with fright.

My husband resumed his hold on the man and walked him to the main road, then accompanied him toward the village, a safe distance from Sunshine Orchard. Paul next hiked back to the Stecks' home and found one of their daughters—Hannah—sleeping peacefully in a hammock under the house (which was on stilts). Knocking softly on the door, he awakened the parents and returned the noodles with an explanation.

The thief never came back, probably greatly relieved to have escaped without harm. After all, compared to the thief, Paul at well over six-feet-tall, must have looked like a giant, although a *gentle* giant.

CHAPTER 25

Twins Soon-To-Be Triplets

Just before we had returned from furlough and moved into our new bamboo home, twins were born at the edge of a river in the jungle. Then the babies' umbilical cords were severed with a filthy machete. These little ones would add to a family of ten children, a family living in poverty without even rice to feed them for the next meal. What were they to do?

Twins meant double care for the mother. And the entire family depended on the mother to search the jungle for their daily food, to gather firewood, to cook for long hours over a hot fire, and to weave the clothing. This could all be done with one baby in a sling; but with two, it was impossible. How could they survive now? The poor mother, who was used to toil and hardship, knowing the helpless situation at home and her physical inability to nurse both babies, silently awaited their doom.

Hearing about the twins, some villagers pleaded with the father to give the babies to them. He, in turn, told his neighbors that their lot was no better than his. The villagers then suggested that the grandmother and an uncle take the infants a day's journey on foot, trekking over the mountains to Sunshine Orchard.

Maria was there to meet the adults with their tiny bundles, a boy and a girl, wrapped in rags, never having tasted their mother's milk. Their small limbs, however, were already bound by devil strings. Maria attempted to convince the uncle to keep the babies, but he shared the impossibility of it all, begging her to take them. How could she say no?

Back from furlough, we arrived at the airport. Maria met us in Old Trusty Rusty with Dan's brother Rick at the wheel, so our daughter could hold the infant twins. We also had loads of luggage and, thus, needed the truck.

Appalled by the babies' horrible condition, we were all soon on our way to a hospital. The twins spent the next twelve days in the neonatal intensive care unit, diagnosed with jaundice and sepsis from the infected umbilical cords. Eventually, they joined the other babies and toddlers in our home.

Life as parents to all these children became an immense challenge for us, accompanied by sleepless nights and continuing childcare during the day. I wore out quickly. One morning while I lay exhausted on my mat in our bamboo home, Maria tried to convince me to go for respite at her hut.

"I'm too tired even to move," I said.

My daughter attempted again to coax me, but without success.

With the twins demanding to be fed every two hours also during the nights, along with preparation of their bottles of formula, changing them, and cuddling the poor babies, there were few moments to rest in between for either Paul or me. And sometimes the noise awakened the other little ones, and they needed attention also.

Suddenly, we heard Eh K'Nyaw's voice as he entered our hut. "There's a father here with a baby. The mother has died!"

Maria looked at me, and together we jumped into action. In that moment our weariness fled, and we actually recognized the situation as somewhat comical—another baby about the same age as the newborn twins!

Within the next few minutes, we tried to convince the father that he should keep his baby. But he remained firm, describing his life in a Karen State war zone. Now without a wife to care for his family's needs and no milk for the baby, the newborn would surely die. The man left no doubt that he would be forced to labor for the Burmese army. So there was no way he could care for this little one whose mother had died a week before.

While Maria began to work on the baby whose health was quickly failing, the father's story soon unfolded. Their village had been attacked at the exact time the baby was due to be born. His whole family had to flee into the jungle to hide while little Kukupaw came into the world under trees during torrential rains. And for a whole month thereafter, the entire family had been running, hiding, and trying to escape the enemy. That kind of exposure and stress had been too much for the worn-out mother. Upon returning to the village after all of the Burmese Army had left, his wife died in her sleep. This left hungry little Kukupaw crying until her vocal cords were overly strained, and no more sound emitted from her puckered little mouth when she tried to cry.

Several weeks passed after we took in Kukupaw before her voice returned. What a precious, squeaky sound to our ears! If I had been asked to describe her initially, I would have labeled her, "a nervous wreck." She spent her first few weeks in hospitals where she was admitted for sepsis. She would become so hysterical that she stopped breathing and had to be given oxygen.

Then miraculously, like a beautiful flower, little Kukupaw eventually opened up and turned into an even-tempered, contented baby!

The constant transporting of patients to a hospital never seemed to end. One day while Maria was tending to chores, she received word that there was a woman who had been in labor for a long time in a nearby village, and she might need to be taken to the hospital. Soon the call arrived for my daughter to come quickly.

Maria grabbed the birth emergency medical supplies and headed for Old Trusty Rusty. She asked someone else to drive the truck, because she decided to stay in the cargo bed with the woman and her husband—just in case . . .

After picking up the couple, their gracious chauffer drove as safely as he could along the winding and twisting country road. The distance to the closest medical center at that time usually took about 40 minutes. As the truck rocked back and forth around corners, Maria realized the baby wasn't waiting. And they were not even close to their destination yet. So she prepared her mind and her supplies for the infant's debut.

As the baby emerged, my daughter noticed the umbilical cord was wrapped around its neck. Releasing the cord, she quickly delivered the lifeless-looking baby boy. Maria caught a glimpse of the father peripherally as she cleared the tiny nose and mouth of mucous. Out came a hearty cry, and the father's huge grin completed that very special moment.

Maria felt greatly relieved and, at the same time, ecstatic, because she had just experienced her first successful delivery—and in the truck bed of Old Trusty Rusty!

CHAPTER 26

"Even the Least of Them"

Paul swept into the kitchen where I was cooking, and he exclaimed, "There's a woman on our porch, and she's green!"

Scurrying out to see her, I searched my memory for some disease that turns the skin green. Then I spotted the poor woman—a miserable sight. Her green skin was raw all over from scratching. Apparently, she had covered herself with some plant concoction in her desperation for relief.

Arriving at a hospital later, I noticed the nurses eyeing their patient with disgust. No one wanted to get close to her. The woman and her child (who was also infected with the same ailment) had hiked over mountains and through jungles from Burma to seek help on our front porch. And this was their first time in a hospital. With the nurses snickering and staring, the mother looked mortified as she observed their crisp uniforms in contrast to the rags she and her child wore. The nurses' critical assessment of her and her little one, both smeared with the green concoction, must have drained any morsel of her self-worth.

Then suddenly, the atmosphere changed when a male nurse arrived on the scene. He displayed exceptional courtesy and tenderness. I watched in amazement as he patiently cared for the woman, even touching her filthy rags and those of her child. In my mind, the man was exemplifying exactly the actions Christ Himself described when He said, ". . . *'Truly I say to you, to the extent that you did it to one of these brothers of Mine, even the least of them, you did it to Me."* (See Matthew 25:40.)

When the doctor came into the ER, he took one look at the sorry-looking twosome and declared, "This is a very serious case!" Without hesitation, he admitted the mother and child. I was immensely grateful they received the care needed—and that our ministry had sufficient funds to pay their hospital bills.

On another occasion, I awoke at 1 a.m., because I was afraid I might miss my wake-up time an hour later. I had to take a three-year-old boy and his mother to the hospital in Chiang Mai. And Emily, needing to go to Laos for visa business, would join me on the trip. The previous night we learned that someone else wanted to come along to the hospital, a man (with Thai papers) who needed only the ride.

The mother and her three-year-old were going to stay with relatives who would help them maneuver through the hospital with its maze-like hallways.

"Are you sure the relatives can do things on their own?" I asked the translator the previous evening in order to guarantee a smooth visit. My linguistic abilities were limited, and the hospital was filled with signs written in a script I didn't understand. Furthermore, to find a Thai person able to help with both English and Karen would not be easy. The translator assured me that the relatives were fluent in Thai.

At 3 a.m. we were ready to leave. Paul had performed a last-minute checkup on Old Trusty Rusty, and then we prayed. Our little patient snuggled with his mother in the back seat. He had a boil the size of a mandarin orange and had not slept because of the pain. But that wasn't the reason we were making the long trip to Chiang Mai. It was because of hydrocephalus, a swelling of the boy's brain and resulting seizures. The local medical staff told us the boy's only hope was surgery in the Chiang Mai hospital.

While still pitch dark, I drove to the next village to pick up another patient. I didn't think much about it until I realized later there were more bodies than expected in the truck bed. And where was the man (with Thai papers) who needed a ride? Perhaps in the darkness I couldn't see him. But soon I was able to count only the forms of two women and two small children.

"Nothing is ever boring around here," I mused.

As we began the climb up the many curvy, steep mountain roads for our seven-hour drive, I started to feel uneasy. Why was the truck feeling different? Why had a warning light on the dash come on? We faced three hours of very steep roads ahead, and now we were losing power as the engine overheated. Should I turn around? No, we had already gone too far.

Lord, You have worked miracles for us before . . . I also reminded Him of the empty fuel tanks in the past and how He had kept Old Trusty Rusty running on—what seemed like—nothing but prayer.

Emily and I also realized we'd be without cell-phone reception for at least the next three hours.

Lord, please keep us going! Don't let us be stranded on this deserted road with these mothers and little ones.

After meeting a hill where I had to put the truck into 4-wheel drive, low, our ride smoothed out, and I sent a silent thank-you prayer heavenward. Later, we arrived in Chiang Mai where the traffic was so intense that the word "crazy" would be its only fitting description. We in Thailand have given motorbikes nicknames, "fireflies" at night and "beehives" in day; they weave in and out of traffic, coming at us from all directions just to buzz us—unbelievable! Thai ladies were often perched on the back, sitting sidesaddle, their legs dangling in dainty sandals or high heels. With no helmets for protection, the riders on the motorbikes dart back and forth, sometimes cutting right in front of us. Alongside this unpredictable traffic, music booms out of bars and other buildings with the volume cranked up as loud as possible.

Despite the noise and confusion, we arrived intact at the hospital in Chiang Mai.

"Where are the relatives?" I asked.

"I don't know," Emily admitted.

The truth suddenly dawned on both of us that I had three women with children depending solely upon me, because no relatives had shown up!

Reluctantly, Emily departed to start her bus travels toward Laos for her visa business.

Lord, what am I to do? Could you, please, send us an angel?

Within the next few hours, my prayers were answered in more ways than just one. I had to keep myself from weeping with joy and gratitude.

First, I left my passengers, who had ridden in the truck bed, to sit in the lobby until they could take care of their business. But if they didn't know Thai either, then—if they understood my bits of Karen and some hand motions—at least they would remain in the hospital lobby until I could fetch them later.

As the mother with her suffering little son and I shuffled from one place to another, we ended up at the wrong office each time. A hospital volunteer (without English skills), who had taken pity on our little patient, motioned for us to follow her. Through the crowds and up different escalators and past various wards, she directed us to another wrong place. But it was exactly where God or His angel wanted us.

One moment, another prayer, and the next moment I heard a familiar voice: "Hi, Lena!"

"Ying!" I cried. "Can you help us?"

She was the perfect person for the hour. Fluent in several languages, Ying had served our friend, Gayle Haberkam, as a translator. Was it a coincidence that this sweet woman had just happened to walk by us in a hospital the size of a small city? Sometimes coincidences are outright, bona fide "divine appointments."

After hearing her story, however, I changed "divine appointments" to "miracles." At the time, Ying worked for the Lord in a mountain village several hours north of Chiang Mai. She was here to visit a friend in the hospital and was supposed to have left the day before. After praying, though, she felt that God would have her stay one more day. She had just decided to pay another quick visit to her friend, then be on her way home.

Because of her friendship with Gayle, Ying was already familiar with this boy's condition. And because she was fluent in Thai, she also knew how to lead us to the correct office. Guiding us through the hospital, dodging people along the way, Ying continued on to an obscure clinic down in unknown parts of a building. (We never would have found the place on our own.)

Leaving us there to await our turn, Ying went to help my other passengers who were seated in the hospital's main lobby. When she returned to us, she took charge of our situation and stayed with us the rest of the day. But even with Ying's help, we ran into one hurdle after another, because the young patient had no Thai papers with him. Neither did he have referral papers from a doctor.

The mother in her torn, soiled sarong sat by her small son, his sling trying to cover his partially naked body full of sores. His bandage was made out of a piece of cloth, and pus and blood leaked out from the draining boil, a staph infection because of dirty water and lack of sanitation was my guess. The mother occasionally wiped the excess onto a piece of her clothing.

Out of desperation, we ended up taking the woman and her son to another hospital. And in the meantime, my other passengers had gone on their way with relatives for which I thanked God (with probably too much enthusiasm in public).

At the private hospital our little patient and his mother were treated as valuable human beings. Soon the tired twosome were directed to the MRI center, then on to the emergency room for the sores and boils to be cared for and dressed properly.

Afterward, we saw a female Thai doctor who took the time to listen to Ying and to evaluate the boy's condition. The physician also seemed genuinely interested in the little guy. We had to pay much more for his care at that hospital, but the boy and his mother were treated well.

After we all ate rice and vegetables that evening, Ying settled the mother and child into a Seventh-day Adventist Church for the night, a little room with mats on the floor to make them feel more at home. She told the mother not to worry, because I would return for the two of them in the morning and take them back to the hospital for their follow-up appointment. Meanwhile, I found a nearby guesthouse for my overnight stay.

Was Ying an angel in disguise? No, she was a real flesh-and-blood person willing to go "the second mile," willing to let go of her plans in order to help a mother and her precious child. Because of Ying staying with us from 10 a.m. till after 7 p.m., I couldn't help but (softly) sing the old hymn, "Just When I Need Him Most." Moreover, I happened to be in need of some optimism in my life during that time, because I was struggling with an unresolved situation. It was like an ulcer, not wanting to heal. This special day with Ying coming to our rescue showed me that in spite of my discouragement, God was near. He was leading. And although we might feel deserted at times, He *will never leave us nor forsake us.*

Old Trusty Rusty lived up to his name and delivered us all home with no more mechanical problems or trouble lights (at least not during that trip over the mountains). Also, the promise above applied to our little three-year-old patient, who today is a teenager, attends a Thai school, and is doing well!

CHAPTER 27

Furlough Miracles

In America for another yearly visa extension, we stayed briefly in the beautiful mountains of Montana. Then we met with Emily who also needed to renew her visa. This otherwise calm and non-confrontational young woman, while riding beside me in the SUV, insisted I should see a doctor immediately. I knew there was nothing wrong with me; but her behavior was so unlike my eldest daughter, who even exclaimed, "Your breathing sounds just like Grandpa's brother who had to undergo triple-bypass surgery!"

She pointed to an Urgent Care walk-in clinic and told me to drive straight into its parking lot and ushered me out of the car while she waited in the vehicle. Upon entering the building, I felt guilty just being there.

When the doctor arrived in the small room where I sat awkwardly atop an examination table, he inquired about my concern. I told him we had been living in a remote area of a foreign country and were home for a visit; but it was my daughter who was concerned and insisted I needed a checkup.

To my surprise, he asked about our location overseas and what we were doing there. After an hour or so of conversation, the doctor asked his wife to come in. He briefed her about our mission in Thailand and told her he thought they should give a couple of their children "a different kind of Christmas"—in Thailand! And right then and there, they agreed to the trip over the holidays to conduct medical mission work at Sunshine Orchard Learning Center and its surroundings.

As I returned with the doctor in tow to our SUV, Emily looked worried. I knew she thought there must be something seriously wrong with me for the doctor to come outside to speak with her. My daughter quickly relaxed, however, and rejoiced with me when she realized how the Lord had set up an appointment for us to meet this Christian physician and his wife. (As promised, the doctor did travel to Thailand at Christmastime with two of his teenage children for a couple of weeks, along with an abundance of medical supplies!)

During that same furlough, we grew weary and in need of another miracle. The visas had to be sent off by the next day. Besides the $1,000 we didn't have for the five of us to apply for the visas, we didn't have the full $2,000 requirement in our bank account either in order to prove that we, as a family, had enough money on hand to support ourselves in Thailand.

Please, Lord, what can we do?

Our solution to this dilemma was to rent a storage unit in a Montana town and use the unit as a venue for a "garage" sale. Our hopes soared, but within a short time we realized something was wrong. Hardly anyone came, and those who did, wanted something for nothing.

At this point my struggle with the Lord went into overdrive. *Father, I feel so hopeless.* (We later learned that it was county fair week, so many people were busy elsewhere.)

Real troopers during the sale, Anna and Josiah worked hard in the hot sun. Because we were all hungry, Paul encouraged me to take our children to a restaurant and bring something back for him. We missed Asian food, so decided to go to a Chinese buffet.

I felt guilty for spending the money, but went ahead anyway. While eating at the restaurant, Anna was using chopsticks and soon caught the attention of an elderly man. He asked where she had learned to eat like a pro. Our daughter told him about our ministry and school in Thailand. Because he was quite interested, she gave him one of our newsletters.

Before he left, the man returned our newsletter, carefully folded, and bid us goodbye. Anna opened up the folded paper and out fell $50! Then upon my visit to the cashier, she informed me that the gentleman, who had been seated near us, had already paid for our meals.

Thank you, Lord! And please bless that man for his kindness.

Within an hour our old horse trailer sold on the Internet for $750, almost enough for our visas. We returned to Paul's parents' house that day with a more positive attitude about our situation.

The next morning we picked up our mail, and there we found an envelope from some dear—but not wealthy—people. Inside was a check for $950 and another check for $350. That was enough, together with what we would make that day during our "garage" sale, to satisfy the Thai embassy requirements.

Tears of gratitude were flowing again. These friends didn't know about our dilemma. But they had been inspired to mail those sacrificial checks to us. As usual, God intervened and proved Himself a faithful Provider.

I wondered if I would ever graduate from His class and learn to trust Him fully, having the "perfect peace" He promised even when obstacles blocked our path and clouds covered every sliver of sunlight.

CHAPTER 28

Timothy's Story

From the time that Timothy, one of our twins given to us at their birth, came into our care, I noticed something like a small open pore on his lower back. It seemed a little strange to me, but because no medical personnel ever mentioned it when we would take him to the hospital, we didn't realize that it should have been a concern.

Timothy had been hospitalized several times for prolonged stays because of meningitis-like symptoms (high fever and chills). But during those stays, the doctors couldn't find the cause, and they failed to diagnose the boy properly.

At two years of age, Timothy developed another on-again-off-again fever. And during that time, he seemed to favor his back, not wanting to lie on it or for anyone to touch it. This time we took Timothy to a hospital in Chiang Mai. The doctor there rushed through the boy's physical, then declared him to be fine except for a mild respiratory infection. About halfway home that evening, we decided to stay the night at a guesthouse. Upon giving little Timothy a bath, I was aghast at the sight of his back. It was swollen in various shades of blue, purple, and red!

I quickly, but carefully, dried off the little fellow, dressed him, and took him to Paul. "We need to return to the emergency room right now!"

Timothy was admitted to the hospital and within a couple of days, he was diagnosed with spina bifida.

There followed one of the most grueling months of our lives. First, a very capable Karen woman was watching our many other children at home during that time. But Paul and I realized she wouldn't remain in good health if she had to continue caring for our babies and toddlers (along with our older children) for another day or two.

Therefore, my husband drove the long way back to our home, packed diapers, clothes, formula, and food for our youngest children; then after a night's rest, he secured all those little ones into Old Trusty Rusty and drove the mountainous route back to Chiang Mai.

Upon arriving in the city, he found an inexpensive, but spacious enough motel room near the hospital for one of us to stay with the babies and toddlers while their brother Timothy underwent pre-op tests, major surgery, then post-op recovery and recuperation.

Meanwhile, I was the designated family member who would stay first at the hospital and act as our son's "nurse's aide" 24 hours a day. With the perpetual commotion in the crowded children's ward, that meant very little sleep for me or for any of the other family members caring for their patients.

Paul and I then took turns between caretaking for Timothy at the hospital and babysitting the many children at the motel room. To save money, we prepared baby bottles and food in that room. Because of the strength and endurance that only God can give, we managed to struggle through our rigorous schedules as caretakers for our youngest children and as nurse's aides for Timothy.

In the midst of this hubbub, somehow the news of Timothy's surgery had reached our friends, Kim and Mark, who had helped watch our children in Thailand during our previous furlough. Kim and Mark were from Australia, but were now working for ADRA and happened to be in Chiang Mai for meetings near the end of our son's month-long hospital stay. So they invited us with all our children to meet them for a picnic lunch at a mountain overlook on Sabbath afternoon.

That Friday finally arrived when Timothy would be discharged from the hospital. At that time, I was told he needed to be monitored by regular hospital visits to make sure his tethered spinal cord didn't stretch too much as he grew, thus causing paralysis. Then while signing our son out of the children's ward, I was immediately "taken hostage" by the head nurse who led me to the cashier's window with the words, "If you don't pay, we will not discharge Timothy."

The nurse's prickly warning along with the sight of the hefty $6,000 bill stunned me momentarily. But I knew there was no way I would leave little Timothy even another hour in the hospital. So feeling somewhat guilty, I dipped into funds earmarked for our new teachers' housing. (This wasn't the first time I had used some of those same funds for Timothy's mounting bills. Each week, the nurse would walk me down to the cashier's counter to pay for Timothy's medicine, or "the boy would go without it." Over the weeks, those bills had totaled $2,000. Added to the $6,000, I then owed the teachers' housing fund $8,000.) God had always provided in the past, so He would surely provide again. Anyway, no guilty conscience could spoil the joy of having Timothy back with all of us in our motel room that evening when the Sabbath hours began!

As planned, the next afternoon Paul, all our youngest children, and I met with Kim and Mark at the beautiful mountain park overlooking the city. After feeding the babies, toddlers, and ourselves, my husband and I found a few peaceful moments to visit with our Australian friends.

It was then that Kim's face lit up with a huge smile as she announced, "Mark and I have raised $8,000 for Timothy's medical bills!"

Grateful tears coursed down my face. God had done it again, this time through Kim and Mark's initiative and some generous donors. Now I could repay the money I'd borrowed from the staff housing funds, so the building project could continue.

In a few days, after the long journey home, we were all settled again near Sunshine Orchard Learning Center. At that time, Gayle

Haberkam had come down from the mountains and was visiting with us while caring for last-minute business before leaving on her furlough.

She found me watching our three toddlers, Timothy, Talitha, and Kukupaw. "Lena," she asked, "would you be willing to help one of the graduates from the school continue her education?" And then she mentioned a certain amount.

I knew all the money we had on hand was in my wallet. And I also carried a list of medicines to buy that very day in order for the Sunshine Orchard Student Mission Team to be able to serve in Karen State across the river. Moreover, I had decided to purchase rain jackets for each member of the team. So it would be a miracle if the money in my wallet would cover even all those items. But Paul and I had long ago resolved never to say "no" to a request such as this, and Gayle's request was not an exception.

Without sharing my monetary predicament, I opened my wallet and carefully counted out the money and, ignoring any nervousness, I handed it over to her. That left only a lone thousand-baht bill (about $30 in U.S. currency) to buy diesel later for our truck. Gayle also needed me to drive her to Mae Sot, so she could take a bus from there to the airport in Bangkok. I silently prayed, surrendering the situation to God.

Later, while driving along a bumpy two-lane road during the trip to Mae Sot, I chatted cheerfully with Gayle, sharing that I had just enough money to put diesel into the truck, but not enough to buy the items on my list. I assured her, however, that I had confidence in God to provide for all our needs, but not a clue how He would do it.

Carefully keeping the truck on the road, I reached into my lap and unsnapped the wallet to show her the thousand-baht bill, then gasped. More bills tumbled out—eight more of them, totaling nine thousand bahts—the very amount I needed to purchase everything on my list! No one had touched my purse or wallet. Those items had been in my possession the whole time since I handed the other money to Gayle. I thanked our heavenly Father for this, another miracle, as my heart sang praises to Him!

CHAPTER 29

The Wedding

We stayed so busy that time seemed to pass at warp speed. Before long, Jordan would soon graduate with his nursing degree, and he and our Maria would be married shortly thereafter in Upstate New York.

Meanwhile, back in Thailand, Maria had moved north of Chiang Mai for Thai language learning. And with so many toddlers and other children, I really missed Maria and her valuable help.

The days continued their swift passing, and I wondered, "Is it God's will for us to attend Maria's and Jordan's wedding in New York?"

Lord, you know we don't have money for our flights . . .

We needed another miracle, this one providing for Paul, Anna, Josiah, and me to return to the United States, not only for the wedding, but also to renew our visas. (Thankfully, Emily would be her sister's bridesmaid and had already saved for her flight.)

We were planning to attend the wedding. But in reality, I knew that unless God intervened, there was no chance of us making the trip. I refused to believe, though, that God would let us down. On the other hand, the money we did save toward our flights kept disappearing. There were the villagers' needs, hospital bills, supplies for the school, and the support for its staff and orphaned students, all adding to a steady outflow.

Father, everything is in Your hands again. If You want us to go, You will have to make it clear by providing the funds.

I thought about my dear mother and my older brother whom I hadn't seen in many years. They were traveling all the way from Sweden to attend the wedding in America. And my brother had even arranged through a friend to borrow a place for us to stay after the wedding. It was a house by a lake, a relaxing venue for all of us to spend precious time together.

Every now and then, my mother or brother would contact me, asking when we would arrive. (They had already purchased their plane tickets.)

I would reply somewhat evasively, "Don't worry! We'll be there." I didn't want to admit to them we didn't have funds for even one of us to fly. The clock kept ticking, and I found myself avoiding the phone, because I didn't want to disappoint my Swedish relatives.

At the same time, Maria also kept asking when we would arrive in New York. Jordan had even mentioned the subject of money. But I knew how many expenses they had, so I told them, "We're fine."

After Sabbath, out of duty, I went through the motions of attempting the impossible, finding tickets for our flights. While my eyes gazed at the high costs on the websites, my friend Abigail messaged, "I heard that Maria is getting married this week in New York. We'll just happen to be in New York at the same time as you'll be there for the wedding. We'd love to see you. When will you fly in?"

"We hope to arrive this Wednesday," I typed back.

Being an intuitive woman, Abigail asked, "What do you mean by *hope*? Don't you have your tickets? *Why* don't you have your tickets?"

I felt perfectly safe in sharing the truth with Abigail, because there was no way she had means to buy tickets, and thus, wouldn't feel guilty about not being able to help. So I simply stated the fact, "We don't have the money."

She wrote back, "Let us know how much you still need. We might be able to come up with something."

How could I tell her how much we still needed? It was thousands! And it seemed a waste of time on my part even to look for tickets, although Maria would be so disappointed if we couldn't attend her wedding. And my mother and brother would be crushed after flying all the way from Sweden. They were also looking forward to meeting Anna and Josiah whom they'd never met. I felt bad, because *in faith* a while back, I had told my relatives we would be there. I wondered, had I finally crossed over from *faith* territory into *presumption* territory?

The next afternoon, the week of the wedding, I spent most of the day in Maria's old bamboo hut, searching the Internet for plane tickets. I felt guilty for neglecting our children—and faithful caretaker, Emily—in our home while I spent the day elsewhere on the computer. The truth was staring right in my face: in order to arrive in New York by Wednesday, we had to leave the next morning for Bangkok. We also needed to keep an important appointment in that city on Tuesday.

As I searched the web, the last-minute cost for tickets had skyrocketed. And with the added need to fly also to the West Coast for visa renewal, my finding affordable tickets was an out-and-out impossibility.

Dear Father, please make a way . . .

As I prepared to set the computer aside so I could return to my other responsibilities, a Facebook message flashed in the corner of the screen. I tapped on the "Chat" button and was surprised to see the name of Abigail's friend who had paid a brief visit to Sunshine Orchard earlier that year. She was a beautiful young woman, barely out of her teen years, traveling around the world. (I had no idea to what faith she belonged, but would soon learn that her heart mirrored Christ's love in a "King-sized" way!)

I blinked, not believing what I read: "Lena, let me buy the

tickets for you. It would be my blessing. Give me your flight dates, your names and birthdates."

Although I'd been praying for a miracle, this seemed unreal. So I explained to Abigail's friend that the four of us needed not only tickets for Bangkok to New York, but from New York to Montana, then later, from Portland, Oregon, back to Thailand. (After Paul and I took care of important business in Montana, my in-laws would drive us all to Portland for our visas, then take us to that city's airport before they returned to Montana.)

Despite the convoluted traveling needs of our family, I saw the words, "Lena, don't worry about anything! It's all taken care of."

Really?

I sat there in that little hut and dissolved into tears. God *was* concerned about us here in the Moei River hinterlands and also about my daughter-the-bride, her fiancé Jordan, and even my family in Sweden! However I praised Him, it sounded trivial compared to what He had just done for us. I couldn't thank Him—or Abigail's friend—enough.

I remember leaving the hut in somewhat of a daze that afternoon. No more searching for the impossible, no more worry! I felt incredibly relieved. And now I could spend some time with the rest of our many children before the trip. But that was not to be, because word came that we were leaving at 7 a.m. the very next day. In a flurry, we told our children, Anna and Josiah, to pack and be ready to go early the following morning.

Arriving in Bangkok the next afternoon, I headed for an Internet café to check if we had the tickets yet. Sure enough! Abigail's friend had, indeed, bought all four of us tickets from Bangkok to New York, from New York to Kalispell, Montana, then from Portland, Oregon, back to Thailand! What she had spent on those tickets took my breath away. I felt paralyzed with indebtedness. How could we ever repay that sum to her?

I immediately messaged our young friend, again expressing our overwhelming gratitude and telling her that we would do our best to reimburse her for such kindness. I didn't tell her of my fear regarding the enormous amount, though.

"Your friendship is pay enough," she replied.

Father God, how can this be true?

My heart felt as if it would swell to bursting with praise to Him for creating such a miracle—and with appreciation to that precious young lady! Once again, we experienced God's faithfulness and were delightfully surprised by a lavishly charitable person who wasn't even a member of our religious denomination. Her graciousness reminded me of the Buddhist, Baptist, and Pentecostal team (a seemingly paradoxical mix of beliefs) that had blessed our ministry with a similar mind-boggling gift.

While still in Bangkok, we shared with a taxi driver about Jesus' love and told him how He always cares for those who call upon Him. The conversation that followed about living by faith impressed the Buddhist man to the point of his telling us that in ten years of driving taxi, he had never experienced such a wonderful time with a family.

Arriving at our destination, Anna quickly snatched one of her beautifully woven "Karen bags" she had made and gave it to the driver. In tears, he refused to charge us for our transportation. (We finally were able to convince him to take the money. After all, he had a family to support.)

All around us, souls are thirsting for the "Living Water" that Jesus offered the Samaritan woman. Of course, Jesus was referring to Himself, just as we should refer to Him. Our personal testimony of His presence in our lives can coax others to take a sip of that spiritual water until it becomes a full-blown waterfall of faith.

With our lengthy flight to New York finished, the few days left before Maria and Jordan's wedding (on Sunday), passed too quickly. But the joy of our reunion with family remained overwhelming as did our gratitude to God and Abigail's friend for making this miraculous window in time possible—which included our daughter, beautiful Maria, exchanging vows with her longtime love, Jordan.

Soon thereafter, the newlyweds returned to Asia. Since then, God has blessed the couple with five children. Today Maria and Jordan, with their family, continue to serve God as missionaries in Thailand.

6

That He Might be Glorified

CHAPTER 30

Trusty Rusty Musty and a New "Chariot"

Old Trusty Rusty had faithfully served us for years. But now the truck would occasionally lose power, the windows failed to close anymore, and the air-conditioning had totally given up.

During the annual water festival, we couldn't roll up the truck's windows, so we were literally sitting ducks! Those open windows were an invitation for people celebrating the festival to pour buckets of water into our open cab. The partiers thought we *wanted* to be drenched. No pleadings for mercy could avert them. Because of the resulting mildew smells inside the truck, "Old Trusty Rusty" soon became known as "Old Trusty Rusty Musty"!

Once when we visited the Chiang Mai Seventh-day Adventist Church, a brother said that our truck looked like an old war vehicle. And we agreed that our battered Old Trusty Rusty Musty did, indeed, look like the victim of war.

At times I felt ashamed of being seen in that old truck. What troubled me was not what people might think of us, but about what our neighbors might think of our God. After all, their Buddha was worthy of their finest abodes—even their finest mobile abodes. I also imagined a question might arise regarding why we cared for so many of "their children," but couldn't provide better transportation for them?

I kept wondering when the "old warrior" would be able to retire and God would provide us with a better, more reliable vehicle. I wondered, too, if our need for dependable transportation was as important to Him as it was to us. I realized that feeding the children and providing for the school were our chief priorities. Was God telling us it was time for us to stop transporting sick people to medical centers?

The day—or should I say, *night*—finally came when the truck died. Paul, Timothy, and I were heading toward Chiang Mai for our boy's checkup on his spinal cord. Left stranded on the side of the highway, Paul quickly realized there was nothing he could do to restart Old Trusty Rusty Musty. With nobody to help us, we prayed. Then my husband started walking in search of water for the radiator.

Paul returned with the highway police who escorted us and towed our truck to the nearest police checkpoint. Then the official took us to a guesthouse for the night.

The next day we boarded a bus and continued our journey to the hospital. Meanwhile, fellow missionaries heard about our plight and immediately sent out an email appealing for funds for a newer truck. Amazingly, funds poured in, and we were later able to go truck shopping!

Of course, we wanted to purchase the very best vehicle the donations could buy. So we spent time going from place to place, in search of something dependable.

Not only were crew cab pickups expensive in Thailand, but also odometers often gave false readings, prompting us to be extra careful in our decision. Before long, some people became impatient, encouraging us to be more zealous in our search for a replacement for Old Trusty Rusty Musty.

Therefore, when we returned from the wedding and visa renewal in the United States, we resumed our vehicle hunt in Chiang Mai, asking God to help us find a good truck quickly. Despite our prayer, we expected the task to take at least a week. So we sent Anna and Josiah ahead on a bus. Quite homesick after our trip to the United States, Paul and I really wanted to return as soon as possible to our many children.

God intervened on our behalf, and before the day was over, we had a truck in our possession. We knew the moment we saw it that this was God's answer to our prayers—a used truck, but like new! (It still had the manufacturer's warranty and other items in the glove box wrapped in their original plastic.)

We headed home in our "new" vehicle and, ironically, arrived before Anna and Josiah on the bus! Our truck was amazing, and we greatly rejoiced for God's gift, so thankful also to those who had sacrificed to make the gift a reality.

One day a "sister" missionary asked to use the truck. We always shared our possessions without hesitation whenever there was a genuine need. But for some reason, this time I felt apprehensive and didn't hand over the keys immediately. I even wondered aloud about the reason for the truck, feeling ashamed afterward for exhibiting a negative attitude. Our friend did need our vehicle for a hospital run, however, and the truck did belong to the ministry, so I relented.

Sadly, our missionary friend and her passengers were involved in an accident on their way back from the hospital. Paul and I left quickly in their vehicle to locate the truck and see what had happened, praying for our friends all along the way.

Arriving upon the scene, we gasped at the sight. *How could anyone have emerged from that wreck alive?* Our beautiful truck lay upside down like a mortally wounded animal, the cab all caved in, and so was the cargo bed.

We were told that the passengers were not dead, but were taken to the hospital. There we learned that our missionary-friend, her two patients, and a translator were all fine and without any injuries!

When the wrecking yard owner saw the truck and learned that the passengers survived, unharmed, he couldn't believe it. Pointing to other trucks with much less damage, he declared (in broken

English) that no one survived those accidents. Then he exclaimed, "The Christian God must be very strong. All those others had Buddha amulets in them, but nobody lived through those crashes."

Nonetheless, we found ourselves without our own transportation—again.

Heavenly Father, You know how much our ministry depends upon a good vehicle, especially for hospital runs . . .

Would we have to wait years for another suitable vehicle for our ministry? We surrendered to God's will again, however, trusting that His timing and plans are perfect.

Not long thereafter, we received an unexpected donation that enabled us to purchase another used vehicle. We were amazed, because it's rare that a donation that large comes in. Furthermore, we soon found a truck identical to the one we lost. It was immediately put to good use for God's kingdom and the unending needs of the people. Thus far, we've not had to nickname the new-to-us vehicle, "Old Trusty Rusty Musty."

CHAPTER 31

Anna

As soon as we first landed in Thailand, Anna immediately blossomed in that foreign field. This was the answer to her heart's need: a life of service and immersion into a unique culture, becoming one with a good-natured, caring people.

Within a very short time, Anna became fluent in the Karen language. She could be seen squatting beside an open fire as she mastered the skills of young Karen women. She could cook the traditional food with amazing haste; and she could weave the finest Karen bags and shirts. Her talented nimble fingers, operating a treadle sewing machine, produced beautiful garments.

At thirteen, Anna was needed for a short time to watch over a severely handicapped young woman (named Kay Ghee) whom Maria had rescued and cared for. But what was supposed to be a temporary arrangement for Anna while Maria cared for an abandoned baby, Anna and Kay Ghee's arrangement instead became a long-term commitment. This began, not as a chore, but a delight as the two young women enjoyed each other's company. Anna was strong and one of few who was able to carry Kay Ghee. Together they were firm believers in a bamboo hut—despite the fact that their dwelling was about to fall apart, and our daughter had to take great care to avoid the many holes in the aging bamboo floor!

Anna was called to leave Kay Ghee for a short time to attend a five-year-old girl in the hospital while the patient underwent surgery. Naw Bee Dah had been like any child in the village inside of Karen State, frolicking around and enjoying the jungle and river. Then one day she fell and stumbled over a rock. Her hip was injured, but it wasn't quite clear to us exactly what had happened. We do know that Naw Bee Dah was taken to a witch doctor for treatment and then to someone giving her massage. When these treatments didn't produce any improvement, her parents took the girl to yet another traditional healer. People pulled and pulled, one to the upper body while others pulled her leg.

Much too late, Naw Bee Dah was brought to Sunshine Orchard for us to transport her to the hospital. There she underwent a series of surgeries. The girl's well-meaning parents, however, didn't understand their need for staying on in the hospital after the operations. Instead, they insisted that their daughter be brought home, back to an unsanitary environment.

Sadly, Naw Bee Dah's large incision soon became infected, and when our students visited her during a "mission trip" to the girl's village, they found her with horrible oozing sores.

Again, we took Naw Bee Dah to the hospital, this time for emergency surgery. Following the procedure, she came to stay with Anna, whom by then—with Kay Ghee—lived in a larger, nicer bamboo hut close to our house. Although only a young teenager, Anna became like a mother to both crippled girls. And each time Naw Bee Dah returned to the hospital, Anna acted as her main caretaker there as well.

The girl continued to walk with a severe limp that was termed a "frog walk" on her hospital charts. But we praise God that today she walks upright, and unless you know her history, you wouldn't notice anything "different" about her.

Nah Bee Dah's surgeon told me, when we returned to him for her checkup, that he was close to tears, because he seldom saw such an incredible improvement as hers. The girl now had complete flexibility and a normal gait.

Naw Bee Dah's older sister came to join her and Kay Ghee at Anna's hut, together with an orphaned child. Anna mothered all these girls who shared her hut for several years there in our lime orchard.

Paul and I often wondered what God had in store for Anna's future when, at such an early age, she had gained so much experience. She even became a desired "medical person" sought after by the villagers surrounding the school.

I admit that traditional academic book study had in some areas been neglected during this time because of the severe needs of those around us. But I wasn't concerned, because Anna seemed to latch onto anything before her and apply herself to learn the proper expertise. And medicine was no exception.

One day, when I asked Anna about how she wanted to further her education, she produced a stack of medical books that a visiting physician had given her. Those large volumes plus books with less impressive jackets, were all marked up with highlighter and were decorated with sticky notes throughout the pages, notes for her attention. I was dumbfounded!

Much like her oldest sister Emily, Anna had always been somewhat reclusive in the way she quietly went about her business without any fanfare. She seemed to need trust and space to blossom.

One day while I enjoyed a pleasant conversation with Emily and Anna, without warning, Anna jumped to her feet and exclaimed, "I can't forget to return the body bag to the mortuary!"

I'm sure I looked horrified. "What body bag?" I asked. "What are you talking about?"

"They have only two of them," Anna explained.

"How do you know?"

With further prodding, Anna opened up to Emily and me about her experiences at local hospitals. Because of superstition, the relatives of those who had died would often not want to handle the dead bodies nor did some of the hospital staff. So we discovered with great surprise that our Anna would take care of those bodies.

The previous week an extremely ill young woman had been brought to Sunshine Orchard, and Anna became her caregiver in the nearest large hospital. After the patient passed away and the relatives arrived at the mortuary to take the young woman's body back to the village, Anna was asked to prepare the girl for her grieving mother to view. Thus, our daughter braided the dead girl's long hair and helped to place the young woman into the body bag. She informed us how they treat the bodies in the mortuary, washing them, placing them in the coolers, etc. During those processes, our Anna became a friend of the mortuary director. And she was concerned, because she needed to return the body bag as soon as possible.

I still felt somewhat stunned by Anna's revelation, but went ahead and encouraged her to return the body bag promptly, as promised.

Today Anna is married to a young Karen man. Naing Win pursued her, and Anna, being a determined lady who was blessed with a sharp eye for true character, had decided that Naing was the one for her. A deep friendship bonded them in marriage and in ministry. Now, with their own children, they serve at Sunshine Orchard Learning Center!

CHAPTER 32

Josiah

Josiah was our "baby," and before we left for the mission field, I felt a large lump deeply imbedded in his neck. With his birth father having died of cancer, I panicked. So Paul and I took our son to a local physician. The doctor's eyes widened when he felt the huge lump, and he went directly to the phone and called an ear, nose, and throat specialist in a larger town.

Later that day my heart plummeted when the specialist informed us that he was sure the lump was cancer, a lymphoma, and Josiah would need surgery immediately. Then he added, "Because of the tumor's position, he might lose the use of his left arm."

After praying, Paul and I decided not to proceed yet with the surgery without first obtaining a second opinion. The problem was that the only other specialist in that area practiced in the same office as the other one!

Lord, the first doctor will be offended. What shall we do?

Meanwhile, we had inquired about some playground equipment someone had advertised. And while we visited that house, the woman there was chatting about how she had been diagnosed with cancer and told that she needed surgery. But she chose to seek a second opinion—and that second doctor saved her from making a huge mistake.

Curious, I asked the name of that second doctor. To my amazement, it was the other specialist in the same office as the one who had told us that Josiah needed immediate surgery! She continued her story and told us that the "second doctor" was a wonderful physician and could be trusted. We felt as if God had spoken to us, because we never asked this woman for advice. In fact, we hadn't even mentioned anything about Josiah.

When we took our son to her "wonderful physician" for his opinion, he assured us not to worry. There was no need for surgery.

"Are you certain?" I asked. "We're leaving soon for a year in Thailand."

He replied in the affirmative.

A year later we returned to this same specialist for another evaluation, and this time the doctor took a biopsy. Again, he told us Josiah was fine.

That "one-year trial in Thailand" stretched to two. And during that time, Josiah's lump seemed to grow—and more lumps appeared in his neck area. So we took Josiah for another biopsy, this time in Bangkok. We could tell the medical staff did a thorough job and, again, we were told there was no cancer.

During those first years in the mission field, Josiah kept suffering from fevers nearly every afternoon, and we worried about him. He later outgrew most of those fevers, and he proved to be quite healthy.

Like Anna, Josiah was fluent in Karen. Probably because of his younger age, however, it took him longer to understand and speak the language than it did for his sister. Therefore, he had a difficult time sitting for long church services without understanding much of the goings-on.

He would say, "Mama, go and read me a story—please!"

And off we would wander to our house, where I'd read him a Bible story. But once he became fluent in Karen, Josiah wouldn't trade his life for anything.

It was important to us for our children to live like the Karen youngsters at Sunshine Orchard. For that reason, Josiah, Anna,

Maria, and Emily didn't have much of what Western children take for granted during their childhood and teen years.

When Josiah would return to America with us for visa renewal, he quietly observed how American people ate such an abundance and variety of foods compared to the Karen. He was astounded by how many different "toys" were available to young and old alike. But our son never seemed to harbor a desire for those playthings, instead remaining content with the outdoor games he enjoyed with his Karen friends. Josiah also appreciated Thailand's natural beauty all around us.

As our family grew, Josiah helped us with the small children. He was fond of them and exhibited endless patience with his younger "brothers and sisters." But soon Paul and I became concerned, because the little ones outnumbered our son; we felt he needed "brothers" nearer his own age. And when the opportunity arose to take in several boys who were boarding at Sunshine Orchard (and were orphans or had been abandoned by their parents for years), we decided to take these four special boys into our family. Soon thereafter, a girl in her teens also needed a home because of health and family problems. In no time, we found ourselves responsible for seventeen children (including Josiah), all living with us in the bamboo hut.

Josiah had, indeed, gained brothers for life. These newcomers proved a real blessing in assisting with the younger children and with other duties in our home. Together they played, worked, and studied. And truly, Josiah was one of them. What a joy to see him later baptized alongside his Karen brothers and sisters!

As a mother, I sometimes worried about Josiah joining activities that required a lot of dexterity and strength. The Karen children seemed much stronger and more limber than our American son. My heart would skip a beat and I'd send up a prayer whenever Josiah would head out with his Karen brothers to swim the swift river, climb mountains with steep, rocky walls, or explore caves that were rumored to contain "bottomless pits."

When Josiah reached his late teens, he would go off on a motorbike with others to conduct branch Sabbath schools in the mountains. Then after much practice, he learned to drive the truck for supplies and for other errands whenever needed.

We greatly appreciate Josiah's calm and steadfast presence behind the wheel. There's no need for anxiety, because he's extremely attentive and we trust him fully.

God also gifted our son with a passion for photography. At first, nature drew his attention. But when we asked him to help us take pictures of student activities, he quickly caught on and realized here was a niche he could fill within our family's ministry.

An interest in videography followed, and he sought to educate himself in producing video reports. As a result, we were able to depend upon Josiah more and more in research and design for various school and church events.

Paul and I are grateful for Josiah's strong commitment to God and for his help in our ministry. We can't thank our Creator enough for the excellent young man Josiah has become.

CHAPTER 33

A Book About 100 Orphans

We lived together in the crowded bamboo hut for three years with seventeen children and youth. It was tight, but cozy, and we all seemed to enjoy our lives there. The bamboo hut had seen its better days and was in need of improvements. Moreover, it was not an ideal situation because of being built too close to the ground, especially during the long rainy seasons. I decided, if we ever had an opportunity to build again and live in a bamboo hut, it would be built high enough off the ground to allow for air circulation, easy cleaning, and serve as a place to hang laundry to dry, even during rainy season.

One day I received an email from a female physician in California, who asked to talk with me. After adjusting for our different time zones, we soon communicated by phone.

Dr. Karen surprised me by sharing how God had placed upon her heart the desire to build a house for our many children and us. I quickly realized she could have chosen any place on the planet. Because she was native to Central America, she surely would want to help a family in her country rather than a family in Asia. But she remained firm in her decision.

Also in the mix was Paul's and my decision not to build a nice place for ourselves and the children until after our school's staff were all in better housing. Actually, at that time, we had been able to start construction on six staff houses, and those permanent buildings would soon be completed.

Dr. Karen then sent us money to start the building of our own new house. Although the six staff homes were all finished by then, we had added more grade levels at our school and, therefore, needed more staff housing for the additional teachers.

The day arrived when our house was finished, and we were excited about moving in. But my enthusiasm was dampened, because surrounding our large new concrete and wood home were tiny rundown bamboo huts with some of our most recent staff living in them. I felt somewhat guilty, because our latest housing situation clashed with everything I held dear.

In my mind there was only one way I could justify our new home, and that was to say "yes" to everyone who needed a place to stay. Soon we had a lot of additional children and youth living inside our new house with us, and life became very complicated. Although I blamed the cement house for the increase in noise, I had to admit that more children meant more noise. And there were forty of them—many teenagers and a herd of little ones!

Before we had left for Thailand years before, Paul and I had read a book called, *One Hundred Orphans*. That book influenced us to have a home where all the children felt loved despite their numbers. If those "adoptive parents" could accomplish that goal with a hundred children, then we should be able to do it with forty, we thought. But within a year, we realized we needed to let at least half of the children go elsewhere—if they had good options. We didn't want to hurt any of them with rejection, so waited on God to make a way without our needing to ask them to leave or for us to remove them.

After lots of prayer, God took care of these extra children, little by little, without harming their self-esteem. And eventually, we again had seventeen children in our home. For us, it was the perfect number. But from time to time, those (who once called our home theirs) return for a visit. Dorm students occasionally stay with us during their school breaks. Also, we are blessed with volunteers who not only live with us, but are an immense help here at Sunshine Orchard Learning Center. Thus, the number of people around our long table varies.

CHAPTER 34

Jaw La Mo

On a busy day while we tried to care for our brood of children, a nice-looking man from across the river in Karen State came to visit. He held a baby, and I realized he was there either to ask for help to go to the hospital, ask for baby formula, or to give us the baby. I held my breath, fearing he would want us to take the little one. I had promised not to take in another baby, because our arms were full since we had received two-month-old Hser Hser Paw, a precious little girl.

The visitor told a story that touched our hearts, a story we knew to be true. A young teenage girl gave birth in this man's village and was unable to care for her baby boy. Then he and his wife offered to take the newborn. They thought the child was beautiful, and they were such happy new parents. Becoming instant parents, however, proved challenging, and the couple found their tasks more difficult than they ever imagined. The baby, named Jaw La Mo, cried a lot and had a hard time drinking. Actually, it took hours to feed the little one just a few ounces of milk. Although the couple loved the child, this gift didn't come without a price. The new mother became ill, and the husband had to stay home to help care for the "demanding" infant. Because Jaw La Mo kept vomiting up the formula, very little nourishment reached his stomach. Even these inexperienced parents realized something was seriously wrong with their little boy.

At that time when the young, weary-looking father came to us from the mountains in Karen State where life was already hard, little Jaw La Mo was over a year old. He had suffered severe brain trauma at birth and his esophagus was malformed, thus causing the difficulty in swallowing. He was unable to sit or do anything. The man admitted they had no strength left to care for Jaw La Mo, and this foster father had to return to work. (His wife was still sick.)

We decided to take the child, not as our own, but in order to help his foster parents and to find little Jaw La Mo another home. We didn't expect this to be very difficult; neither did we realize how very taxing the care of this child would become.

Not too long after the foster father's departure, we loaded the little guy into our "new" truck and headed to the nearest orphanage. The staff there said they were too full already and couldn't take him. After a few phone calls, it started to dawn upon us that placing this handicapped child in a caring home was going to take a miracle. We even traveled to the city and everywhere we went, doors closed to Jaw La Mo. So we brought him home to do our best to care for him until God found a way.

Our Emily took the baby for the evenings and early mornings, then also for the weekends. We had the little guy during the nights—until Emily demanded to care for Jaw La Mo fulltime (probably for our welfare).

Next, a Karen girl offered to help with the baby during the day until school started. Caring for Jaw La Mo took much time, and none of us had any to spare. Emily had formed a bond with the child, and soon he surprised us all with beaming smiles at her and her only. He noticeably felt peaceful in her arms. And with the patience of a saint, our daughter figured out how to feed him milk without it coming back up—one drop at a time!

Dear Father, what shall we do? School will soon start . . .

When our Karen helper told us she had to return to school the following morning, we received a call from a physician friend in Mae Sot.

"The day after tomorrow I will meet you in Bangkok," she said. "A home is there for handicapped children, and they're willing to see Jaw La Mo."

The next day we left on the journey, a long drive that included an overnight stay at a guesthouse. Then Emily, Jaw La Mo, and I were to meet our doctor-friend at a bus stop in Bangkok. The bus stop had no name, or she didn't know its name. All our friend could tell us was, "It's a place where buses stop on their way to the main bus station near the old airport and close to a movie theater."

Anyone familiar with Bangkok would know those directions were not at all helpful. But after praying about our dilemma, we left the guesthouse and headed north toward where I thought the old airport to be. And in no time we found ourselves quite lost. Praying for God to make a way, we continued off the highway onto side streets, stopping once in a while to ask for directions—but to no avail because of our limited ability to speak Thai.

Stopping again, I spotted a Caucasian-looking man in an outdoor café. Entering the place, I asked him if he knew the area. "Yes," he said, then proceeded to speak to me in *Swedish*, my mother tongue! I was flabbergasted. God brought just the person into my line of sight, the only person I could understand perfectly.

Receiving excellent directions, we were soon on our way again. I was elated by this time, feeling God's hand guiding us to meet up with our friend, who—from time to time—would call my cell phone, assuring us she was on her way although her bus was running late.

The Swedish man had told us to make a U-turn to reach the bus stop. But traffic spread across six lanes. Should I keep to the left or to the right? So again, I stopped to ask for directions, this time at a fruit stand, where people stared at me blankly, not understanding English.

Suddenly, a van pulled out from a side street, the driver hollering for me to follow him.

How would he know where I'm going?

No time to argue or question, because he was already heading out into the hectic traffic. Jumping back into our truck, I tagged after him. He rolled down his window and hand-signaled for us to go over a bridge and do a U-turn in that chaotic place. Then we spotted the buses, taxis, cars, and people.

"Emily, there it is! But how are we going to find a parking place among such a crowd and with this much traffic?"

At that very moment, our friend phoned and exclaimed, "I'm here. I just stepped off the bus."

As we peered through the truck window, there she was—all smiles! We never needed to find a parking place, after all; I simply slowed way down and let her hop on board our vehicle. God is mighty and amazing, even in Bangkok's wild traffic!

Arriving at the orphanage, I admit to apprehensive feelings, because we had heard horror stories about orphanages in big cities. And by now, we loved this little boy, and no way would we leave him in a bad situation. Immediately, however, I realized this place was a dream come true. I don't even have words to describe it, except "bright and cheery." There were only fourteen children, and about ten women were on staff to care for them.

When our doctor-friend introduced us to the caretakers, one of them exclaimed, "I want to see the baby! I had a dream last night in which I saw the baby that God would send us. I want to see if this is the one in my dream."

As soon as she looked at little Jaw La Mo, tears welled up in her eyes, and I felt tears in mine, too. They had told us they usually wouldn't take any more children. But after the dream episode, they welcomed the little boy with willing arms.

In no time, Jaw La Mo was immersed in a loving home environment. And after a feeding tube was inserted, I was surprised to see his hunger quickly satisfied without his losing it all and having to start over again with hours of effort. Of course, Emily and I wept, because it was difficult for us to leave the little fellow. We were satisfied, though, knowing that we could return anytime to visit.

Again, God had proven Himself faithful, and we went on our way, rejoicing through our tears.

CHAPTER 35

Ponderings in the Night—And Day

The steady beat of drums vibrated throughout our Sunshine Orchard campus—noise from a nearby celebration. They were not the sounds of heavenly music. Quite the contrary! But with that constant beat, beat, beat, I wondered, would our young people still be drawn to their gentle Savior or to the noise and confusion of this world? Would our Karen children and youth understand the critical contrast between outward frivolity and the gospel's simplicity?

Heavenly Father, when the call comes for some of them to move to the city, what will they do? Will they leave our school for a concrete jungle filled with the same kind of noise and worldliness? Most important, will they remember Jesus? Will they remember to call upon Him who laid down His life for them? Will they continue to make Him their bulwark and trusted Friend?

It was almost midnight, but the so-called "music" was still pulsating with such intensity that we couldn't escape from it. In our home, however, a computer was playing a Nebblett Family CD to surround our senses with some semblance of divine peace while our children tried to drift off to sleep.

Carefully maneuvering around a few of the older boys, who at that time, usually didn't display much outward interest in spiritual things, I smiled when I noticed they were sleeping close to the computer that played the soothing CD. My heart was also touched when I realized they had given up their mosquito nets just to be near the "heavenly" music.

That night as sleep refused to come easily, I felt overwhelmed with gratitude for Paul and me to have been privileged to help establish Sunshine Orchard Learning Center and for us to have called this beautiful place alongside the Moei River, "our home and our mission." And this mission would not have come to fruition if Erik had not given up several months of his life long ago in order to teach me from his old, worn Bible. That elderly gentleman had exhibited boundless patience with me as we delved into the depths of Scripture.

Feeling my face redden with remorse, I recalled how sassy I must have sounded to Erik while challenging him with such questions as, "How can Christians believe that unrepentant sinners—who, maybe, lived for only 60 years or a little more—have been burning in hellfire and will continue to burn forever and ever? God is supposed to be fair and just, and that's horribly unjust!"

"You're right," he replied. "That would be horribly unjust. But let's look at what God's Word really says about the subject."

Starting with the creation of Adam, Erik read Genesis 2:7, "*Then the LORD God formed man of dust from the ground, and breathed into his nostrils the breath of life; and man became a living being.*"

As he walked me through more of the Bible verses in the creation story, I read aloud how the devil (in the form of a serpent) had lied to Eve about the forbidden fruit on "*the tree of the knowledge of good and evil.*" The serpent contradicted God, telling Eve, "*You surely will not die,*" if she ate that fruit.

I could still remember the profound sadness I felt when I read how such a blissful paradise, free from pain and sickness, was lost not just to humanity's first parents, but to all generations thereafter, including mine and beyond. And for the first time, the tragedy of death entered our world. The *breath of life*, which had made man *a living being*, depended upon Adam's and Eve's obedience to God. So when they trusted Satan instead of trusting their loving Creator, God would eventually withdraw that *breath of life*, causing their deaths— and also limiting the lifespan of all their future descendants.

Erik next dismissed me with an assignment: to look up the word *death* in my concordance, and from there, find references to how the Old Testament and even Jesus in the New Testament defined that "sad word."

Back at my apartment, I quickly discovered that the Old Testament described the deaths of David, his son Solomon, and other kings as *sleep*. Even the Books of Job, Jeremiah, and Daniel called death a *sleep*. In the New Testament, Jesus Himself called the death of Jairus' daughter, "*sleep*." The Lord also said his friend Lazarus was "*sleeping*" when, in reality, His friend was dead. I found it comforting that Jesus did not correct heartbroken Martha when she told Him that she expected her brother Lazarus to live again "*in the resurrection at the last day*," (see John 11:24, NKJV).

By the time I returned to my weekly study, I had found over 50 places in the Bible that described death as *sleep*. Moreover, I told Erik that the Bible probably wasn't describing an "ordinary sleep," but "a mysterious state of unconsciousness" that, in all likelihood, only God fully understood.

My elderly mentor then gave me more verses to read aloud, describing the sleep of death, such as Psalm 146:4, "*His spirit departs, he returns to the earth; In that very day his thoughts perish.*"

After several other texts, he asked, "Lena, where are those who truly lived for God and, before they died, were awaiting the promised Messiah? And what about those born after the birth, death, and resurrection of Jesus? If they sincerely accepted Him as their Savior (even at life's end) and lived for Him during their remaining years, days, hours, or minutes, but are also dead at this time—where are they now?"

Upon scanning my notes, I replied, "Apart from a few exceptions mentioned in the Bible, they're *sleeping*. Even the saintly Stephen, who was martyred for his faith, is *asleep*, according to Acts 7:60."

Erik's voice turned somber. "And what about the wicked dead, those who have never repented and turned to God? Where are they now?"

"They, too, are sleeping in a mysterious unconscious state," I said. Then I exclaimed, "And that means, they haven't been burning all this time in hellfire!" (So . . . at least in part, my original question had been answered.)

Erik paused before asking next, "Besides the fact that the *wicked* dead are not being tortured in hellfire all this time, why do you think it's important to know that truth—and that the *righteous* dead are also resting in their graves in a type of *sleep* until Christ's Second Coming?"

I didn't need to ponder his question for long, because I'd already been considering people who claimed to communicate with the dead, like at séances or at a fortuneteller's table. "Erik, I've run across about a dozen places in the Bible, thus far, that warn against evil *divination* and so-called *mediums* calling up *familiar spirits* (supposed dead people). There are also warnings about *witchcraft, wizards, sorcerers,* and other forms of *spiritualism*; and all of those are defined clearly in God's Word as *abominations* to Him."

After turning some pages in my Bible, I continued, "I now know that the spirits of dead people are not alive at this time. But the Bible does reveal that the devil and his evil angels—or demons—certainly are alive!" Finding the fourth chapter of Matthew, I continued, "In fact, right after Jesus was baptized by his cousin John in the Jordan River, the Lord ventured farther into the wilderness and was tempted by Satan. Of course, Jesus won that contest with quotations straight from the Scriptures." Before Erik could respond, I wondered aloud, "But what will happen eventually to God's followers . . . and also to Satan's followers?"

It was then that my mentor decided to expand our study to the *resurrection of life* and the *resurrection of judgment* (meaning, *condemnation*), as spoken of in John 5:29. He also showed me other verses that told of a thousand-year gap between those two resurrections—"or the *Millennium*, as many Christians call that time period," he said.

Regarding the *resurrection of life*, Erik quoted I Thessalonians 4:13 through 18, emphasizing verses 16 and 17 of that passage: "*For the Lord Himself will descend from heaven with a shout, with the voice of the archangel and with the trumpet of God, and the dead in Christ will rise first. ¹⁷ Then we who are alive and remain will be caught up together with them in the clouds to meet the Lord in the air, and so we shall always be with the Lord.*" (What a comfort those promises would become in the future, and they still are for my children and me, knowing—without any doubt—that our Eddie will someday awaken from his "sleep in Jesus" and immediately behold the Savior returning to our planet!)

Besides the texts describing the *first resurrection*, Erik added other promises, such as Jesus' words found in John 14:1 through 3, "*Do not let your heart be troubled; believe in God, believe also in Me. ² In My Father's house are many dwelling places; if it were not so, I would have told you; for I go to prepare a place for you. ³ If I go and prepare a place for you, I will come again and receive you to Myself, that where I am, there you may be also.*"

I then learned from Revelation that those Christians in the first resurrection will spend a thousand years, safely with Christ in Heaven. During that time, the wicked dead (still "asleep" in their graves) will be judged, leaving only Satan and his evil angels with no living humans on our desolate Planet Earth—nobody to tempt for a thousand years! It was then that Erik decided to send me home with additional verses to read, so we would have more to study during our next session.

Thanking him for providing answers to my many questions— and for the meal—I packed up my Bible and thick notebook and headed out the door and to the elevator, already eager to learn more the following week.

CHAPTER 36

To and from the Tunnelbana

Not too long after the night of disturbing "music," I sat near the sleeping mat of a precious, sick child. I suddenly heard him stir. Rinsing and twisting cold cloths, I applied them to the boy's feverish brow, neck, and chest. Sitting him upright, I coaxed him to sip more of an herbal drink I'd made and cooled earlier that evening. As he settled back down and drifted off to a more restful sleep, I breathed another prayer for him, then returned to reminiscing about my first adventures in God's Word.

When my next Bible study arrived, I was treated again to the same vegetarian meal Erik always served. After we cleared the table, he said, "Lena, we've already established that the *dead in Christ* and those *who are alive and remain* at the Second Coming will rise and *meet the Lord in the air*. Now, can you tell me when the wicked dead will finally be resurrected?"

"At the end of the thousand years, known as the Millennium," I replied.

"True! And faced with every one of their unconfessed evil deeds recorded accurately in the books of Heaven, the wicked will have no choice but to agree that God is fair and just," Erik predicted. "Also, I believe even Satan and his evil angels will admit to the fairness of

God. And here's why: Philippians 2:10 and 11 contain a beautiful promise, . . . *so that at the name of Jesus every knee will bow, of those who are in heaven and on earth and under the earth, [11] and that every tongue will confess that Jesus Christ is Lord, to the glory of God the Father.*"

It was then that my usually calm teacher became animated when he repeated, "*Every* knee will bow, Lena, and *every* tongue confess! The only time *every* knee will be able to bow and *every* tongue be able to confess—along with *all* other beings ever created, including Satan and his evil angels—is after the Millennium. That means, never again will doubt remain in the universe regarding the fairness and justice of God!"

Our discussion turned back to how Jesus proved God's sacrificial love on Calvary's brutal cross. Then Erik and I explored the final scenes of the great controversy between Christ and Satan in Revelation 20:7 through 15 (KJV). I felt terribly sad when I read that those people *not found written in the book of life* will be *cast into the lake of fire* along with the devil and his evil angels.

When the old gentleman noticed my changed expression, his voice took on a note of sympathy. (And did I detect that he choked up with emotion? Noticeable tears filled his eyes as he hastily pulled out a handkerchief, drying his eyes and nose.)

"Lena, if you'll bear with me, you'll soon discover that in the lake of fire there is justice and, yes, even mercy. So let's find the answer to your original question that led to this study. What about those unrepentant people as well as Satan and his evil angels? Will they be given *eternal* life, to suffer *forever* in that lake of fire?"

Mulling over all the latest verses on the subject, I hesitated for a few moments before answering, "Well, the wages of sin is *death*—not life!"

Erik agreed, pointing out, "In Revelation 21:8, God Himself defined the *lake that burns with fire and brimstone . . .* as *the second death.*"

His voice sounded especially sorrowful as he maneuvered me

through what would happen to those whose names will not be *found in the book of life*. First, he read Jude 7, describing Sodom and Gomorrah's destruction by *"eternal fire."* Then he asked me, "Are Sodom and Gomorrah still burning today?"

"Of course not!" I exclaimed. "That fire happened many years ago."

"Yes," Erik said. "And that fire burned until both cities and everything and everyone in them were completely consumed. We see the proof of that in 2 Peter 2:6, where the apostle depicts God *reducing* those two cities *to ashes*. Ashes mean nothing and nobody at all were left."

Then he thumbed through his Bible to Matthew 25:41, reading where the King shall say to those on his left hand, *"'Depart from Me, accursed ones, into the eternal fire which has been prepared for the devil and his angels.'"*

Next, he introduced me to another synonym for the word *eternal* and that was *everlasting* where the King James Version of the Bible describes the word, *hell*, in Mark 9:45 as a *fire that never shall be quenched*. "An everlasting or *unquenchable* fire," my mentor pointed out. Then he referred to Jeremiah 17:27, where God warned about that type of fire that would *devour the palaces of Jerusalem and it shall not be quenched*—if the Israelites didn't obey Him.

"Then, Lena, way over in Jeremiah 52:12 and 13, God kept His word. Babylon's captain of the guard did set fire to Jerusalem until everything was completely burned up. And that's when the fire that *shall not be quenched* went out!" Erik exclaimed. "Again, *unquenchable, eternal, and everlasting,* all mean the same thing: the *results* of an *unquenchable* fire are the same as the *results* of those other two synonyms," he said, "because not even that *unquenchable fire* is still burning today."

Erik sighed, then leaned back in his chair. "And so, Lena, the time will arrive when the prophecy in Ezekiel 18:4 will come true: *The soul who sins will die.* In Matthew 10:28, Jesus made it quite clear that both the *soul* and the *body* will be destroyed *in hell*." Next, Erik read Malachi 4:3, "'*You will tread down the wicked, for they will be ashes under the soles of your feet on the day which I am preparing,*' says the Lord of hosts." (Again, he emphasized the word, *ashes.*)

Many Psalms have comforted me, but not the Psalms Erik selected that afternoon decades ago, ones that finalized the fate of the wicked: . . . *But all the wicked He will destroy* (Psalm 145:20); *But the wicked will perish*; . . . *They vanish—like smoke they vanish away* (Psalm 37:20); . . . *and fire will devour them* (Psalm 21:9).

Explaining that "the king of Tyre" symbolized Satan, Erik then read about that "king" in Ezekiel 28:18 and 19: ". . . *Therefore I have brought fire from the midst of you; It has consumed you, And I have turned you to ashes on the earth.* . . . *¹⁹* . . . *And you will cease to be forever.* And that will include Satan's evil angels," Erik said, "because of what we just read in Psalm 145:20, that *all the wicked He will destroy.* And Revelation 20:15 also includes all the wicked people who ever lived on Earth: *And whosoever was not found written in the book of life was cast into the lake of fire,*" he repeated.

Erik and I both sat in solemn silence for several moments as we contemplated all we had studied that afternoon (which was fast turning into evening). Then I heard his soft voice. "Lena, how does Ezekiel 33:11 describe a quality of God's character?"

I found the verse and read, ". . . *As I live, saith the Lord GOD, I have no pleasure in the death of the wicked.* . . ." (KJV).

Erik explained how God has no choice. He realizes that if the cancer of sin and sinners isn't completely eliminated from Earth and, thus, the entire universe, sin will again raise its ugly head and re-contaminate His creation. "Peter prophesied, *But the day of the Lord will come like a thief, in which the heavens will pass away with a roar and the elements will be destroyed with intense heat, and the earth and its works will be burned up*" (from 2 Peter 3:10). He continued, "The fire that will destroy the devil, his evil angels, and all those people *not written in the book of life*, that fire will also purify the earth from sin." Then he asked, "What does Revelation 21:1 say will happen after that purifying fire?"

"*Then I saw a new heaven and a new earth,*" I read, "*for the first heaven and the first earth passed away, and there is no longer any sea.*"

We then discussed the beautiful prophecy of the *new Jerusalem* coming down from Heaven—and how God would dwell with His people on Earth—"sort of coming full circle from the Garden of Eden *before* sin polluted our planet," Erik suggested.

Next, he asked me to end our study on a "brighter note" by reading aloud Revelation 21:4, which I did: "*And He will wipe away every tear from their eyes; and there will no longer be any death; there will no longer be any mourning, or crying, or pain; the first things have passed away.*"

That evening as I walked to the *tunnelbana* in Stockholm, I scarcely noticed the dusky sky above. Lost in deep thought, I felt an overwhelming relief to have discovered that not one person, not even Satan and his evil angels, would suffer forever and ever in hellfire. Instead, the Bible confirmed that even Satan would *cease to be forever* (Ezekiel 28:19). No more evil!

As the underground train continued along its route toward the suburbs where I lived, not even an inkling of curiosity entered my mind that night regarding the chapters in Daniel that Erik had assigned for our next session.

Because Psalm 34:8 says, *O taste and see that the Lord is good,* I now can honestly describe those next studies as absolutely *delicious*!

CHAPTER 37

Mene, Mene, Tekel, Upharsin

My patient's brow no longer felt hot. I breathed a sigh of relief, because this little one—although not of my flesh—was etched on my heart as if he were my own son. To make sure his fever had broken, I carefully inserted a thermometer under his arm. Smiling when I saw that his temperature had finally fallen below the 100-degree mark, I whispered, "Thank you, Lord!" Then again, I coaxed the little guy to swallow more of the herbal drink. Although he was probably out of danger, I stayed by his mat throughout that long, sleepless night, returning to my memories of studying the exciting Book of Daniel.

Back at my apartment, when I began the first chapter of Daniel in the Bible, I understood at once that God Himself was behind Judah's downfall to the heathen nation of Babylon. In fact, God allowed Babylon's King Nebuchadnezzar to march straight into Jerusalem, besiege that city, and defeat King Jehoiakim of Judah. From there the story expanded to some young Hebrew captives, Daniel and his three friends, who were later re-named Shadrach, Meshach, and Abednego; and all of them were carried far from their beloved home country to a foreign land.

Then when I met with Erik for our study, we discussed how Daniel and his companions (tactfully) objected to consuming the king's meat and wine. They asked the *prince of the eunuchs* if they could try an experiment of sorts, substituting a simple diet of *vegetables and water* instead of eating the king's rich foods and drinking his wine. God blessed those Jewish captives with robust health. In fact, the Bible says, *they were fatter than all the youths who had been eating the king's choice food*! (See Daniel 1:15 through 20.)

Then I found it interesting that according to Genesis 1:29, man's original diet also included simple foods: *every plant yielding seed that is on the surface of all the earth, and every tree which has fruit yielding seed; it shall be food for you.* I later discovered it wasn't until after the Flood that meat was added to the human diet. God next divided those flesh foods into "clean" and "unclean" categories (see Deuteronomy 14:2 through 5). God even gave Moses specifics in that chapter (verses 6 through 8) on how to determine the differences among the animals. Our Creator also presented a more detailed list in Leviticus 11—specifying in verses 9 and 10 which *fish* are good for food.

Revealing to Erik why I had become a vegetarian, I described how horrified I felt when I'd witnessed people clubbing fish to death! Then I added, "Something interesting I discovered at that time, though, was that I began to pay more attention to what foods are healthy for me and what other practices are best for my health, like getting enough exercise and sleep, avoiding alcohol or any kind of other drugs that might cause harm to my body—and my good judgment."

Erik looked pleased. "Your referral to 'good judgment' reminds me of the warning in 1 Peter 5:8, *Be of sober spirit, be on the alert. Your adversary, the devil, prowls around like a roaring lion, seeking someone to devour.*" Then he said, "Remember, Lena, eating all the right foods and practicing other good health habits are not the main key to Heaven. Only Jesus' sacrifice on the cross and our positive relationship with Him are what count when it comes to our salvation, which is a *gift* and not something we've *earned*."

Then my mentor asked me to read I Corinthians 3:16 and 17,

which I did: *"Do you not know that you are a temple of God and that the Spirit of God dwells in you? 17 If any man destroys the temple of God, God will destroy him, for the temple of God is holy, and that is what you are."*

"Lena, you've already mentioned alcohol and certain drugs causing our bodies harm. So I don't need to give you the list of Scriptures that point to alcohol as turning people into *babblers* and causing all sorts of trouble. But if you look at I Corinthians 6:9 and 10, there's a list of people who *will not inherit the kingdom of God.* And among them are *drunkards.* But does that mean that alcoholics and drug addicts or any of the other sinners mentioned in that list cannot enter Heaven someday?"

I shook my head. "If they repent and ask the Lord to forgive them of those sins, and they live for Him, then they will go to Heaven someday."

I was quiet for a few moments, then said, "I've witnessed so much suffering because of alcohol and illegal drugs. I still have memories of my own parents' divorce because of my father's alcoholism. And he died much too early. Also, as I've grown older and been out in society, I've witnessed child neglect, crimes, disease . . . such incredible heartache because of alcohol and drugs. I can now understand how most of those tragic circumstances probably stem from people not treating their bodies as *the temple of God* and keeping *the Spirit of God* dwelling *in* them."

Then I asked, "But, Erik, what about tobacco?"

"Smoking cigarettes and cigars—and chewing tobacco—are other habits we should avoid to keep our bodies healthy and our minds clear," he told me. "Lena, in my vocation as a minister, I've visited many people in hospitals who were actually dying from lung disease; but still, they were so addicted that they asked others to fetch their cigarettes and matches for them! That's why it's so important not even to try those products in the first place."

We discussed further how living healthfully also helped us live closer to God and to be open to the Holy Spirit's promptings. Erik next asked me to read aloud the sections of Daniel where his Hebrew friends were tested.

I was fascinated as I continued to read from the Book of Daniel. In the third chapter, the faith of Shadrach, Meshach, and Abednego was tested when the Babylonian King Nebuchadnezzar erected a huge statue of gold. Then he decreed that whenever his subjects heard certain musical instruments sound, those people were to fall down and worship the golden image. He also warned that if anyone did not worship the statue, that person would be cast into a burning furnace.

As I read, I wondered where Daniel was, because he was absent from his friends when the king's music sounded and Shadrach, Meshach, and Abednego defied the royal order, continuing to stand. So off those three went to the fiery furnace!

But as the king peered into that furnace, he exclaimed, *"Look! I see four men loosed and walking about in the midst of the fire without harm, and the appearance of the fourth is like a son of [the] gods!"* (See Daniel 3:25.)

Of course, after that amazing occurrence, Shadrach, Meshach, and Abednego were released, unharmed. *"A son of [the] gods* is interpreted as *the son of God* in other translations," Erik said. "And if those other translations are correct, which many theologians believe they are, that mention (by a then-pagan king) of the Messiah many centuries before He would be born in Bethlehem is remarkable, indeed!"

Later, King Nebuchadnezzar himself would also fall upon hard times. Because of pride in his magnificent building projects and because of his neglect of the poor, the king was suddenly struck by a weird mental disorder (probably what psychologists now call, "clinical lycanthropy"). Nebuchadnezzar believed himself to be a *beast of the field* (even eating grass). Meanwhile, his regents took over the king's governmental duties—until the monarch came to his senses seven years later and was able to rule again. But, oh, how he repented! This once proud king cried fervently, *"Now I,*

Nebuchadnezzar, praise, exalt and honor the King of heaven, for all His works are true and His ways just, and He is able to humble those who walk in pride." (See Daniel 4:37.) That former pagan king truly became a believer in the one-and-only God.

I couldn't help but reflect upon my own conversion from, essentially, knowing nothing at all about God. I, too, had been an unbeliever like that biblical king. I didn't wander around in fields and eat grass like Nebuchadnezzar, but I did come to recognize the "King of Heaven" as being real and more than worthy of my praise. Then contemplating about what I had read, I told Erik, "I think all of us are just as pitiful as that poor, insane king before we come into a saving relationship with our Creator."

Continuing, I read on. When the king's relative Belshazzar succeeded Nebuchadnezzar, that royal grandson did not worship the true God. In fact, he was very much in the devil's court when he held a great feast and served his family and other guests wine in vessels stolen from *the house of the Lord of heaven*! When Belshazzar faced frightening disembodied fingers writing a mysterious message upon the palace wall, however, his knees began knocking together. (See Daniel 5:6.) Such news brought the queen into the hall to inform Belshazzar about the prophet, Daniel, who could interpret the strange writing.

Summoned to the event, Daniel courageously interpreted the mysterious message for the king, *MENE, MENE, TEKEL, UPHARSIN*: "*God has numbered your kingdom and put an end to it.* [27] *. . . you have been weighed on the scales and found deficient.* [28] *. . . your kingdom has been divided and given over to the Medes and Persians.*" (See Daniel 5:25 through 28.)

As prophesied, that very night, King Belshazzar was slain, and Darius *the Median* (meaning, Mede) took over the kingdom. Moreover, one of the first official acts of the new king was to appoint Daniel the chief of three *presidents* who, in turn, ruled over *120 princes* in Darius' kingdom.

Daniel proved to be the best and most popular among all the

appointed rulers, and that popularity bred envy among the other rulers. Consequently, those envious men tricked King Darius into signing a decree: . . . *Anyone who makes a petition to any god or man besides [the king] for thirty days, shall be cast into the lions' den.* (See Daniel 6:7.)

Did Daniel abide by the king's decree and change his practice of kneeling and praying toward Jerusalem three times a day, thanking God? Not only did the prophet continue his prayer routine, but, as always, he performed that routine before his open windows! (I recalled how touched I was by Daniel's faithfulness, and I decided I wanted his kind of faith for myself. Silently, I'd asked God for help in meeting that spiritual goal.)

I then read how the plotters immediately informed the king about Daniel's disobedience to him. Darius spent hours trying to find a legal way out of his predicament, but failed. So Daniel was cast into the lions' den just as surely as his three Hebrew friends had previously been cast into the fiery furnace at the direction of a different king. Darius then sealed the den's covering stone with his royal signet.

The king felt miserable, and after a sleepless night, he rushed to the lions' den and *cried with a troubled voice . . . "Daniel, servant of the living God, has your God, whom you constantly serve, been able to deliver you from the lions?"* (See Daniel 6:20.)

"O King, live forever!" came the prophet's voice from inside the den. Another of God's special people was miraculously protected. (See verse 21.)

My mentor then brought out a clean sheet of paper and laid it upon the tabletop. Curious, I watched him draw a good-sized image of a man, his arms folded across his chest, and his entire body standing straight and tall in the center of the page.

With a gleam in his eyes, Erik said, "Lena, during our next study, we are going to examine the stunning prophecy found in Daniel 2, a prophecy that has mostly been fulfilled at this time. There's only one part of the prophecy that hasn't come true yet.

Your homework is to go home and read the second chapter of Daniel several times until you've become quite familiar with it. . . . And don't forget your notebook!"

And with that directive, he dismissed me until our next meeting.

CHAPTER 38

A Powerful Prophetic Dream

At last, my little patient was out of danger, so I was able to settle down on my sleeping mat beside him and try to catch a few hours of sleep before all of the household awakened. But the excitement I had felt many years before returned, along with more memories, and kept me awake a while longer . . .

Upon reading the 49 verses in Daniel 2 several times throughout the week, I could hardly wait to board the *tunnelbana* and head back to Erik's apartment. I ate his tasty meal as fast as I could without seeming impolite, then helped him clear the kitchen table. (Although I had read the entire Book of Daniel even before these studies began, I was still eager to hear my mentor's viewpoint on Daniel's interpretation of King Nebuchadnezzar's mysterious dream.)

After the dishes were cleared away, Erik retrieved the picture of a large man (whose arms were locked across his chest), the picture he had drawn the week before, and laid it again on the tabletop.

Then upon praying for guidance, he said, "Lena, in ancient times, dreams were taken very seriously. Although King Nebuchadnezzar couldn't actually recall the details of his nightmare when he awakened, he did remember that it had caused him great distress.

Therefore, the monarch demanded that *the magicians, the conjurers, the sorcerers and the Chaldeans* tell him what he had dreamt the night before—and what the dream meant."

Erik looked over at me and asked, "How did the king's so-called wise men respond?"

"The same way I would have!" Opening the Bible to Daniel 2:4, I read the second part of that verse, ". . . *Tell the dream to your servants, and we will declare the interpretation.* Then the Chaldeans bantered back and forth with their ruler until we learn in verse 12, King Nebuchadnezzar grew furious and told his captain of the guard (Arioch) *to slay the wise men of Babylon.*"

"And who were among those wise men, Lena?"

"Daniel and his three Hebrew friends were among Nebuchadnezzar's wise men; but the prophet was able to persuade the king, to *give him time, in order that he might declare the interpretation to the king.*" (See Daniel 2:16.)

"What faith!" Erik exclaimed. "Then Daniel joined Shadrach, Meshach, and Abednego (also named Hananiah, Mishael, and Azariah), praying for God's mercy regarding the king's dream. . . . So, tell me, Lena, how did God answer their prayers?"

"God gave Daniel *a night vision* that revealed Nebuchadnezzar's dream and its interpretation," I replied.

"Correct! Now notice in verse 19, *Daniel blessed the God of heaven.* But, Lena, he didn't stop there. He continued to praise and thank God in wonderful ways throughout verses 20 to 24!" Erik suddenly looked sad, saying, "I wonder how many times God has answered my own prayers and I've forgotten to thank Him?"

I nodded. "Something else I realized, Erik . . . In the presence of a pagan king, Daniel boldly gave all the credit for the dream's revelation and interpretation to *God in heaven.* And, amazingly, God actually made *known to that* pagan *king, Nebuchadnezzar, what will take place in the latter days.* In other words, what would happen down through the centuries in our own future!"

Grinning his approval, my teacher continued, "And now, please read in Daniel 2, starting with verse 32, Daniel telling the king what he actually saw in his dream about a large *statue . . . whose appearance was awesome.*"

I could hear Erik using some sort of drawing implements on his picture atop the table as I read: "*The head of that statue was made of fine gold, its breast and its arms of silver, its belly and its thighs of bronze, 33 its legs of iron, its feet partly of iron and partly of clay. 34 You continued looking until a stone was cut out without hands, and it struck the statue on its feet of iron and clay and crushed them. 35 Then the iron, the clay, the bronze, the silver and the gold were crushed all at the same time and became like chaff from the summer threshing floors; and the wind carried them away so that not a trace of them was found. But the stone that struck the statue became a great mountain and filled the whole earth.*"

"You can stop there," Erik said.

I then looked over at the drawing he had made the week before. The man's head was now a golden color; the chest and folded arms were silver; the belly and thighs were a reddish brown; the lower legs were a dark gray; and the feet were covered with dark and light splotches of gray.

"And now for the interpretation, Lena . . . What does the end of verse 38 reveal about the head of gold?"

"Daniel very plainly told King Nebuchadnezzar of Babylon, *'You are the head of gold,'*" I said.

Then Erik took a wooden ruler and used it to draw a long line, left to right, straight through the image's neck, and nearly to the paper's other edge. Next, he printed *Babylon* on that line to the left of the golden head.

"Lena, in world history over the centuries, there have been a lot more empires or kingdoms than just the ones referred to in Nebuchadnezzar's dream. I believe the reason God highlighted these particular kingdoms was because they ruled over God's special people, the Jews, whether they remained in Israel or were exiled to a foreign country (as Daniel and his friends were)."

Next, Erik continued to use the ruler to draw another line, that one under the man's silver chest and folded arms; the next one under the reddish-brown (representing bronze) thighs; another one under the dark-gray portion of its legs (through the ankles); and a last line drawn under the image's feet.

"Historians differ," he said, "about the exact year that the Babylonian Empire came into power over Israel, speculating anywhere from 626 B.C. to 605 B.C. So, to be safe, let's use the oldest date." He then printed *626 B.C.* on the line to the right of the golden head. "One thing historians do agree on, Lena, is the splendor of the Babylonian Kingdom with its hanging gardens, its massive walls, and its great wealth—undoubtedly why Babylon was represented by a head of gold in Nebuchadnezzar's dream."

As I looked again at the golden head of Erik's drawing, he requested that I silently review Daniel's interpretation in verses 32 and 33—which, he said, has proved to be a prophecy of actual succeeding kingdoms that arose after Babylon, covering many centuries beyond Daniel's life!

Then my elderly friend asked, "Of what metal were the *breast and arms?*"

"Silver," I replied.

"Lena, do you remember the strange writing on the wall in the fifth chapter of Daniel?"

"Of course!" I exclaimed. "And even more strange were the fingers attached to nothing, writing a warning to King Belshazzar!"

"Yes," Erik agreed, "and that night Babylon fell to Medo-Persia and King Darius." Then my teacher wrote *Medo-Persia* on the line to the left of the silver chest and arms—and on their right, he printed the year *539 B.C.*

"Just as silver was of lesser value than Babylon's gold," he continued, "what was the next metal on the image, of a lesser value than silver?"

Erik was already writing *Greece* to the left of the image's reddish-brown mid-section and thighs when I said, "Bronze."

"Alexander the Great of Greece would conquer the Medes and Persians at the Battle of Arbela in 331 B.C.," he said, "and would remain in power until 168 B.C. when Rome took over." Erik then wrote *331 B.C.* to the right of his drawing's mid-section and thighs that represented Greece.

"Lena, how did Daniel describe the fourth kingdom?"

"It would be as strong as iron and, later, that chapter described iron as crushing and breaking things," I said.

Erik nodded. "Rome—sometimes quite brutal—would rule for over 600 years and be the empire in power when the Messiah was born in Bethlehem and throughout Jesus' ministry and His death on a Roman cross," Erik noted, adding, "and also during the time of Jesus' Resurrection and His Ascension to Heaven!" Then my teacher wrote *Rome* on the line left of the image's iron-gray lower legs. On the right, he wrote two dates instead of just one: *168 B.C. to 476 A.D.*

"What about the image's feet and toes?" I asked.

Erik smiled. "To me, this begins the most fascinating part of the dream, probably because it refers to the origin of some of our ancient ancestors! Would you read, Daniel 2:41 through 43, Lena?"

I, too, had found that part interesting, but questions still lingered about what the verses meant. Then I read, *"In that you saw the feet and toes, partly of potter's clay and partly of iron, it will be a divided kingdom; but it will have in it the toughness of iron, inasmuch as you saw the iron mixed with common clay. ⁴²As the toes of the feet [were] partly of iron and partly of pottery, [so] some of the kingdom will be strong and part of it will be brittle. ⁴³And in that you saw the iron mixed with common clay, they will combine with one another in the seed of men; but they will not adhere to one another, even as iron does not combine with pottery."*

Erik took in a big breath before beginning his commentary: "When the Roman Empire started to decline in power around 476 A.D., it wasn't because of another empire or kingdom taking over. Instead, it was because of an invasion of ten barbarian tribes." Then he read from a list: "The Ostrogoths, Sueves, Burgundians, Franks, Lombards, Visigoths, Alemanni, Vandals, Herules, and Anglo-Saxons. . . . Interestingly, seven of those tribes evolved into seven countries that are thriving today as Europe!"

Leaning back in his chair, he continued, "Through many means—royal marriages between countries and even wars—leaders have tried to recreate the former Roman Empire; but as Daniel 2:43 prophesied, ". . . *they will not adhere to one another, even as iron does not combine with pottery.*" Then he wrote *Europe Divided* to the left of the toes and printed *476 A.D. to Present Day* on the line to the right.

"That's amazing!" I declared. "The entire dream-prophecy is absolutely amazing. And only God could have known Earth's future across those many centuries—and so precisely!"

It was at that moment I discovered how my faith had grown even more during that study. At the same time, I realized that my tender regard for Erik had grown as well. Over the months, I'd been impressed by his intricate knowledge of the Holy Scriptures, how he always knew where to find just the right Bible verse or verses to answer any of my questions.

Looking over at him, I noticed his white hair, thick glasses, and his eyes, still the color of a Swedish summer sky. I also took note of the tremble in his huge hands. How I appreciated the unselfish effort he had exercised as my spiritual mentor! I was certain that God Himself had chosen that elderly gentleman as the instrument to guide and anchor me in Bible truths.

Turning back to the large drawing on the table, I asked, "What will happen next, Erik?"

"Well, why don't you look into the New Testament portion of your Bible and tell me what I Corinthians 10:4 says?"

Finding the place, I read the Apostle Paul's words concerning the Jews' journey under the leadership of Moses: "*and all drank the same spiritual drink, for they were drinking from a spiritual rock which followed them; and the rock was Christ.*" (I suddenly realized again, here was another reference to the Second Person of the Holy Trinity—akin to the reference by King Nebuchadnezzar—this one referring to Moses' era, about 1500 years before Christ was born in human form!)

"Now hold that thought, Lena, and look again at what you read earlier in Daniel 2:34 and 35."

I had read about *a stone cut out without hands that struck the statue on its feet of iron and clay and crushed them.* I'd also read about all the components of the image (*the clay, the iron, the bronze, the silver, and the gold*) being *crushed* and becoming *like chaff* on *threshing floors*, then being *carried away* by the wind so *that not a trace of them was found.* Then the *stone that struck the statue became a great mountain and filled the whole earth.*

Erik then shared his thoughts about the verses I'd just visited again. "Lena, I believe that stone might very well be a reference to the Rock, Jesus the Messiah, about whom Paul wrote in I Corinthians. And that Rock (or Stone in Nebuchadnezzar's dream), made *without* (human) *hands*, will—at the end of Earth's history do away with any worldly governments (thus, turn them into *chaff* that the wind will carry away)—then set up God's Kingdom here on this planet. And the *great mountain that filled the whole earth* reminds me of Mt. Zion where the Jewish Temple stood."

Then my mentor beamed as he told me, "Wait till we study all the components of the Temple, Lena, and how those components pointed to the Father, Son, and Holy Spirit—and especially to how Jesus would be our Kindred Redeemer!"

My dear teacher then looked me squarely in the eyes. "But for now . . . remember, Lena, Revelation 21:2, where the Apostle John saw the holy city, *new Jerusalem, coming down out of heaven from God, made ready as a bride adorned for her husband*? That means: no more earthly kingdoms to fall prey to new conquerors (as we've seen in Nebuchadnezzar's dream)—or to be invaded by barbarians. That final kingdom will last for all eternity with Jesus as our King!"

At that point, I couldn't help but think, *And no more barbarians, like Satan and his evil angels, preying upon people. . . .*

Then Erik closed his Bible, promising, "In the future, Lena, we'll study more of Daniel—and about the Jewish Temple. But for next week, please read God's Ten Commandments in Exodus 20:2 through 17 and Moses' review of them in Deuteronomy 5:6 through 21.

With that assignment, I was cordially dismissed.

CHAPTER 39

The Best Till Last

Our little guy looked pale a few hours later, but I was grateful his fever had fled by sunrise. Keeping a houseful of children quiet, so my patient could sleep a little longer, was impossible. Therefore, with everyone dressed, we began the day with a morning devotional, breakfast, and the melodic voices of most of our youngsters as they headed out the doorway to school.

After my exhausted-looking child promptly fell asleep again on his mat, I used the free time to do some chores, then relaxed for a few moments. Again, my mind returned to Erik's huge influence on my spiritual life.

Resuming our Bible study, he and I discussed all of the Ten Commandments except the fourth one. When I inquired about it, he simply said, "We're saving the best till last."

Finally, Erik asked me to read that Fourth Commandment in Exodus 20:8 through 11, which I did: *"Remember the sabbath day, to keep it holy. ⁹ Six days you shall labor and do all your work, ¹⁰ but the seventh day is a sabbath of the LORD your God; in it you shall not do any work, you or your son or your daughter, your male or your female servant or your cattle or your sojourner who stays with you. ¹¹ For in six days the LORD made the heavens and the earth, the sea and all that is in them, and rested on the seventh day; therefore the* LORD *blessed the sabbath day and made it holy."*

Then my mentor asked, "What's the first thing different in this Commandment, compared to the others?"

I quickly responded with, "The word, *Remember!*"

"Can you guess why God used that word?"

"Well," I ventured, "the Israelites had been exiled in Egypt for over 400 years, and they were slaves at least during a portion of those years. I doubt that slaves were allowed to take a day off for the Sabbath. And many of those Jews must have forgotten all about God's day of rest during their captivity."

Erik looked pleased by my answer, then added, "Also, as our Creator, God knew how busy we humans would become with our daily lives down through the centuries; you might say we would become *slaves* to our jobs and other responsibilities. He wants all of us to *remember.*"

Then my elderly friend switched his focus. "I know Christians who insist that the Sabbath Commandment was made just for the Jews. But according to Scripture, that's not entirely correct. Let's turn back to the beginning pages of Genesis. What did God create on the sixth day, Lena?"

I found Genesis 1:24 and reviewed that verse through verse 31 before replying, "On the sixth day, God created all the animals. He also made humans on that day." I then read verse 27, *"God created man in His own image, in the image of God He created him; male and female He created them."*

"Now, Lena, what does Genesis 2:2 say?"

"By the seventh day God completed His work which He had done, and He rested on the seventh day from all His work which He had done."

Erik then pointed out, "If God had simply rested on that day, then perhaps future generations would have been justified in doubting the holiness of the seventh day. But the Bible goes on to report in Genesis 2:3, *Then God blessed the seventh day and sanctified it, because in it He rested from all His work which God had created and made."*

Erik knew that I had read the entire Bible already, so he asked me about the miraculous deliverance of the Jews from their slavery in Egypt. "Lena, did you notice, once the Jews were free to practice their faith again, that God expected them to keep the Sabbath?"

Noting my furrowed brow, he continued, "Look at Exodus 16:4 and 5. It's where God promises He will rain bread from Heaven for the Jews to gather *a day's portion every day*. But then *on the sixth day* . . . it was to *be twice as much as they* gathered *daily*."

"Yes!" I said with some excitement. "And instead of the worm-infested leftover bread—or *manna*—smelling horribly rotten on the seventh day (as any leftovers would have on other days of the week), the *manna* they gathered on the sixth day, stayed fresh for eating on the Sabbath."

"That's right," Erik agreed. Then in a tender tone he continued, "Those poor people had been captives in a pagan land for so long that God had to treat many of them like children as He re-introduced His laws to them." Next, he asked, "Did you notice that this particular lesson, regarding the Sabbath in Exodus 16, took place *before* God actually wrote the Ten Commandments with His own hand on tablets of stone on Mt. Sinai?"

I nodded. "That's true. Also true, though, were the doubters in Exodus 16:27, those that went out on the seventh day to gather, they found nothing." Then I asked, "But, Erik, why do most Christians—including ours here in Sweden—hold their weekly services on the first day of the week instead of the seventh day?"

I felt disappointed when Erik announced, "That's a good place for us to stop our study, Lena. You have a whole week to look up *first day* or *first day of the week* in your Bible, your concordance, and commentaries; then you can return and tell *me* where in the New Testament Jesus or even any of His disciples made that change in the Sabbath from the seventh day of the week to the first day."

I almost floated out of his apartment, because I loved solving a good puzzle. But that mood quickly faded when I opened my concordance later and was surprised to find that the New Testament mentioned "first day of the week" only eight times—and the first five references concerned the day of the week that Jesus rose from the dead (see Matthew 28:1; Mark 16:1-2, 9; Luke 24:1; and John 20:1). And to my dismay, none of them stipulated a change in the Sabbath Commandment. I did note, however, that Sunday (the first day of the week) began at the *end* of the Sabbath, according to Matthew and Mark.

Next, I looked up the sixth text, hoping this one (John 20:19) would provide the clue as to why the Sabbath was changed to another day of the week: *So when it was evening on that day, the first day of the week, and when the doors were shut where the disciples were, for fear of the Jews, Jesus came and stood in their midst and said to them, "Peace be with you."*

That had to be the proof text of the disciples' first worship service, commemorating Jesus' Resurrection on the *first day*. Then the section, where the disciples were assembled *for fear of the Jews*, caught my attention.

Backtracking to Mark 16:14, I noticed where Jesus actually reproved the apostles at that time, *because they had not believed those who had seen Him after He had risen.* (See also Mark 16:9 through 13, where the disciples believed neither Mary Magdalene nor *the two*, whom I guessed were the couple of travelers that Jesus had joined on the road to Emmaus.)

As hard as I might try, there was no way to twist those texts into a celebration of Jesus' Resurrection on the first day of the week. Instead, it was a gathering *when the doors were shut where the disciples were, for fear of the Jews.*

The disciples weren't commemorating the *first day of the week* because of Jesus' Resurrection; His followers were plainly frightened and hadn't even believed the reports about His Resurrection!

The next-to-the last "first day" text, Acts 20:7, stated, *On the first day of the week, when we were gathered together to break bread, Paul began talking to them, intending to leave the next day, and he prolonged his message until midnight.*

Thinking this was, indeed, a Sunday service, I made sure by consulting my commentaries and other reference books, where I discovered the biblical way of determining the day of the week. Each day began at sundown and continued until the next sundown (which reminded me of the days of Creation in Genesis where *the evening and the morning were the first day*). That meant Paul's meeting occurred on Saturday night, not Sunday night. Furthermore, Paul continued talking with them a long while until daybreak, and then left. (See Acts 20:11.) It soon became obvious to me that those Troas Christians were spending every last minute with their beloved Paul. Preaching through midnight till very early Sunday morning must have been an exception.

To make sure, I found other examples of Paul's preaching services in Acts 13:14, 42, 44; 16:13; 17:2; and 18:4. In fact, to Jews and Gentiles alike, Paul preached on the Sabbath day. And he didn't preach only in synagogues on the Sabbath, but also at Philippi: *And on the Sabbath day we went outside the gate to a riverside, where we were supposing that there would be a place of prayer . . .* (Acts 16:13). Thus far, no place was the Sabbath said to be any other day than the seventh.

I was then down to my last first-day verse, I Corinthians 16:2, *On the first day of every week each one of you is to put aside and save, as he may prosper, so that no collections be made when I come.*

My mood picked up again when I concluded that this sounded like offering time when collection plates were passed around during church services—*upon the first day of the week*—Sunday! But what was Paul's real concern here? Apparently, believers in Jerusalem were in great need. And as Paul traveled, he was collecting funds for those needy Christians. So the apostle advised other believers *to put aside and save* (meaning at home) their special offerings *upon the first day of every week,* so those special funds would be ready when he arrived in their area. The apostle wasn't speaking about a weekly church service in this context.

I sat there feeling stunned as I asked myself, "How can most Christians around the world keep the first day of the week as *holy* when God Himself *rested on the seventh day . . . and blessed the seventh day and sanctified it*, and He even placed it near the center of the Ten Commandments?"

Then I wondered how and when and why that change occurred? Hoping Erik would have the answers, I eagerly looked forward to our next study.

When that afternoon arrived, he greeted me with a broad grin. "So, Lena, did either Jesus or any of His disciples change the Sabbath from the seventh day to the first day of the week?"

As we made our way to the kitchen, I said, "Not Jesus—and not even one of His apostles or other disciples made any kind of change to the Sabbath Commandment in Exodus 20."

Placing my Bible and book bag on a nearby chair, I continued, "I thought maybe the latecomer-apostle, Paul, would have made some sort of change to the Sabbath, but no! Not only did Paul go to the Temple (or synagogue) on the seventh-day Sabbath, but he also worshipped out in nature, beside a river, with other believers on that day."

As we ate lunch, Erik added another component to my study, "Lena, Christian friends have told me they worship on Sundays, because, according to the New Testament, they are now under grace and no longer under the law. Jesus, they say, nailed that law to the cross."

My heart sank. "Now you tell me, just when I'd made up my mind about keeping a seventh-day Sabbath as God ordered us at—and even before—His appearing to Moses on Mt. Sinai."

Erik shook his head. "Don't worry, Lena! Everything we need to know about this, we'll find in the Scriptures. When we finish eating, we'll discover the truth."

Soon my Bible, a commentary, and a few other reference books had taken their places on the cleared table.

Then Erik handed me a page on which he had written various Bible texts. "With this being a somewhat controversial subject, let's look at the texts my well-meaning friends have used to *prove* to me that God no longer expects us (His Christian people) to keep the seventh-day Sabbath, but the first day of the week as His day of worship."

As I scanned the page, I noticed a column of verses that seemed to show the other side of the subject.

Erik next asked me to turn to the Book of Galatians in the New Testament, because his "Sunday-keeping friends loved Paul's epistle to the Galatians to prove their side of the controversy," he said.

As requested, I read Galatians 3:19, where Paul states the purpose of the law: "*It was added because of transgressions, having been ordained through angels by the agency of a mediator, until the seed would come to whom the promise had been made. . . .* That does sound like since the Seed, Jesus, has come, the law is no longer valid!"

"It does *sound* that way," my mentor agreed, "and so does Galatians 4:9 and 10, in which Paul actually scolds the Galatian Christians for turning *back again to the weak and worthless elemental things, to which you desire to be enslaved all over again? ¹⁰ You observe days and months and seasons and years.*"

I wondered if Paul was talking about *days* like the Sabbath, especially when Paul used the examples of Hagar and Sarah. "In throwing out the *bondwoman* in Galatians 4:30," I asked, "wasn't that apostle advocating throwing out Mt. Sinai's covenant, the Ten Commandments?"

Erik remained his usual patient self, so I, too, tried to be patient when he asked me to read Colossians 2:16, which I did: "*Therefore no one is to act as your judge in regard to food or drink or in respect to a festival or a new moon or a Sabbath day.*"

Finally, I couldn't keep quiet any longer. "That sure sounds like Paul was throwing out those laws—even the Sabbath days," I said.

"If so, then why the contradiction by Jesus in Matthew 5:17 and 18?" I read aloud, *"Do not think that I came to abolish the Law or the Prophets; I did not come to abolish but to fulfill. ¹⁸ For truly I say to you, until heaven and earth pass away, not the smallest letter or stroke shall pass from the Law until all is accomplished."*

Erik responded at once, "I know this sounds as if Paul and Jesus are at odds about keeping the law—especially because of the Lord's words, *until heaven and earth pass away.* But let's continue and see how God's Word solves this seeming puzzle. What does Romans 3:23 say, Lena?"

I read, *". . . for all have sinned and fall short of the glory of God."*

"And how does 1 John 3:4 define sin?" he asked.

I already knew that verse by heart in the King James Version. *". . . Sin is the transgression of the law."*

Erik then recited Romans 3:28, *"For we maintain that a man is justified by faith apart from works of the Law.* In other words, Lena, Apostle Paul was saying here that it's not *doing* the law that saves us, but it's *having faith* in what Jesus did for us on the cross—and with His Resurrection from the grave—that saves us! Lena, read the best part about our salvation in Ephesians 2:8."

"For by grace you have been saved through faith; and that not of yourselves, it is the gift of God." I smiled, echoing what my teacher had said during an earlier session: "Our salvation is a *gift.* It isn't something we need to earn."

I still had my finger in Romans 3 and noticed verse 31: *"Do we then nullify the Law through faith? May it never be! On the contrary, we establish the Law."*

Erik added another important point from James 2:20, *". . . faith without works is useless."*

I smiled again, concluding aloud, "So what this is saying is that I shouldn't keep the law *in order* to be saved, but *because* I am saved."

Erik nodded. "And 1 John 2:4 makes this all quite clear with, *The one who says, 'I have come to know Him,' and does not keep His commandments, is a liar, and the truth is not in him."*

Next, he read Colossians 2:14 through 17 from the King James Version, repeating verse 14, *"Blotting out the handwriting of ordinances that was against us, which was contrary to us, and took it out of the way, nailing it to his cross."*

My teacher then explained, "This is where some Christians have gotten the Fourth Commandment law confused with *ceremonial* laws (special *sabbath days*)." He explained further, "When the *Seed*, the true *Lamb of God* (the Messiah, Jesus) was born on Earth, then died for all humanity—past, present, and to come—and rose from the dead, then those *ceremonial* laws were no longer needed. Way back then, those types of laws, or *ordinances*, all looked forward to Jesus, our Savior; thus, those types of *ceremonial* laws are now *nailed to the cross.*"

Then Erik's words took on a more earnest sound. "But, Lena, the original Day of Rest, initiated in the Garden of Eden, then later expressed on Mount Sinai as the Fourth Commandment, is still viable today. In fact, for a surprise, read Isaiah 66: 22 and 23!"

I hurriedly turned to Isaiah, reading aloud, *"'For just as the new heavens and the new earth, Which I make will endure before Me,' declares the Lord, 'So your offspring and your name will endure. ²³ And it shall be from new moon to new moon And from sabbath to sabbath, All mankind will come to bow down before Me,' says the Lord."*

I beamed, realizing that we humans will still be a part of special worship services on every Sabbath—for eternity!

Erik's study on law and grace, along with my private research of all the *first day of the week* texts in the New Testament, drew me back to my original question: "I still don't understand why most Christians are keeping Sunday as the *Lord's* special *day* when the Fourth Commandment plainly says the *seventh day* was the one God Himself *blessed and sanctified.* And no place in all the Bible was the seventh-day Sabbath abolished or replaced by a first-day Sabbath." I looked into my teacher's compassionate face. "Tell me, Erik, how did that change happen?"

"My answer requires quite an investigation into ancient history,

Lena. So we'll need to wait another day for that . . . maybe next week?"

Already feeling eager for the following study, I packed up and headed again for the *tunnelbana*.

CHAPTER 40

An India Experience

Our little boy had recovered and was, thus, able to accompany the rest of our large family to the Sunshine Orchard Chapel for Sabbath school and church. Moreover, this Sabbath would become extra-special, because after the worship service, our visiting pastor would conduct baptisms in the nearby Moei River.

Beyond today's calm waters still loomed Lay Klo Yaw Mountain, standing as tall as it did when, years before, our first groups of students and school staff had escaped in a canoe across the then-turbulent river to safety here on Thailand soil. My heart felt as if it could soar to that mountaintop while I watched some of those same youngsters, now much older, begin lining up to dedicate their lives to God on that serene summerlike day.

More students were arriving for the anticipated service, and I noticed even a few shy onlookers from the village at the outskirts.

Because the pastor was still back at the chapel, and all our own younger children stayed near Paul and me, I continued to linger off to the side, enjoying a shady spot and reminiscing more about how God had used Erik long ago to start me on a path to this very place.

So much time had passed, however, since those wonder-filled journeys into Scripture that I couldn't remember everything he taught. But I did recall Erik reminding me of the ten barbarian tribes that had invaded what is now Europe. And along with those tribes, some erroneous beliefs had crept into the Christian church of that time.

Sun worship was one of those beliefs. The Roman Emperor Constantine wanted to unite the former sun-worshippers—who had converted to Christianity—with other Christians who were still worshiping on the biblical seventh-day Sabbath found in the heart of the Ten Commandments. Therefore, in A.D. 321, the Emperor instituted the first of several civil-religious Sunday laws, granting Roman citizens, who lived in cities, a day of rest "on the venerable Day of the Sun."

Then in A.D. 364, the Roman Catholic Council of Laodicea passed its first ecclesiastical Sunday law. Denouncing the practice of resting on the biblical Sabbath, the church substituted resting on Sunday instead. As Erik and I opened the pages of Daniel again, I learned that A.D. 538 was an exceptional year, because it marked the beginning of Daniel's 1260-year prophecy. That exact date (538 A.D.) was when the Roman Catholic Third Council of Orleans also issued an even stricter Sunday law, ordering agricultural workers also to rest on the first day of the week, so they could attend church.

I recalled how tenderly Erik spoke of his Catholic and Protestant friends who kept Sunday holy instead of God's Sabbath, which (he reminded me) was instituted first in the Garden of Eden, then literally set in stone on Mt. Sinai. He said he prayed for the Holy Spirit to reveal the truth to his friends, so they, too, could enjoy the beautiful rest and renewal of God's special day.

And then, after months of study, I had discovered for myself that not only had Jesus kept the seventh-day Sabbath from Friday sundown to Saturday sundown, but also His disciples kept that same Sabbath—even after Christ's Resurrection! And today His Sabbath still remains near the center of the Ten Commandments, a memorial to God's mighty creative—and His *re*-creative—power in us, His Christians, through the Holy Spirit.

At long last, there came an afternoon when I declared to Erik, "I want to be baptized in a Seventh-day Adventist Church!"

Looking puzzled, he asked, "How did you arrive at that conclusion?"

"By studying the Bible—and a book about different denominations." I also told him I had found three Protestant churches that worshipped on the seventh-day of the week, but only one of those churches believed *all* the truths I'd discovered in God's Word (thanks to Erik's help, of course).

That was when the elderly retired evangelist, who had become a special friend, made plans for me to be baptized in a Seventh-day Adventist church a few weeks later. Meanwhile, I was busy making my own plans to fulfill a longtime desire to care for orphans in a foreign land.

Although I had been brought up in an atheistic environment, from an early age I had felt a hefty tug on my heart—a desire to help children in Asia. Moreover, a few months before my decision to get baptized, I had written to the Christian directors of an orphanage in India. And then I received a reply, welcoming me as a volunteer for their mission. They needed more help with translating and writing sponsor thank-you letters (not exactly what I had envisioned myself doing in India, but I was excited and grateful for the opportunity to serve).

As alluded to near the beginning of this book, the day finally arrived when I was baptized in a small Swedish Seventh-day Adventist Church. Just after the pastor said, "I baptize you in the name of the Father and of the Son and of the Holy Spirit," he immersed me completely under the water; then as he lifted me up, an "Amen!" chorus resounded throughout the congregation. Friendly Christians later lined up after that inspiring service and welcomed me to "the fold." One particular man shook my hand, then whispered in my ear, "Remember, don't look at people, but keep looking at Jesus!" I believe his advice has helped me stay close to my Savior over the many years since that special event.

On the very next day after my baptism, I boarded a plane to India. And when I joined that India ministry, I was caught by surprise at the differences in our Christian beliefs. Although I explained why I kept the same Sabbath as Jesus and His disciples did and, therefore, prepared for it by cooking and cleaning beforehand on Friday, those Christians didn't understand; in fact, they tried to talk me out of my beliefs. And they were even troubled by my vegetarian diet—especially by my not wanting to eat the pork they served. Although I showed them in the Bible where God considered pork one of the "unclean" foods we shouldn't consume, I'm sure they saw me as a misguided "babe in Christ."

At the same time, I was impressed by the sincere, strong faith of those believers. Many of their everyday activities came to shape my life forever. Late into the night, I would listen to the prayers of the "aunts" who assisted in the ministry. Also, upon each of their excursions—short or long—everyone would gather and encircle the person or persons leaving, then pray for "God's protection, blessing, and guidance."

After some time, I accompanied a small group of them, which included "Grandpa," the ministry's spiritual head and patriarch, on a train journey up into the steep mountains of India. We were to help at a children's home in Darjeeling. On our way there, we were told to disembark and board another train. Then we had to wait for hours on that train. Finally, we learned the cause of our delay—a horrible wreck with numerous deaths on the very train that went on without us!

With sad hearts, our group hired a taxi to take us up the narrow, winding mountain roads to our final destination. Upon our arrival, a wide-eyed "Grandma" welcomed us with tears of gratitude. She had heard about the train accident and feared we had all been killed. (I was deeply touched by the obvious love on display between Grandpa and his wife when they were reunited.)

After a much-needed rest, I met two other visitors, women who were missionaries from Bhutan and Tibet. They were to lead evangelistic meetings in an old barn on that mountain mission complex. Despite the barn's lack of electricity and, thus, a lack of sufficient lighting, the well-attended meetings still lingered long into each night.

After dark one evening when the two women finished their talk, the pastor ("Grandpa") made a call, "If you want to receive the Holy Spirit, please raise your hand, and we will come and pray for you."

What happened next still remains vivid in my memory. Because I desired the infilling of the Holy Spirit, I raised my hand. At the same time, although I respected the staunch faith among those dear people, some of their actions had troubled me. So I prayed silently, "Dear Father, in Jesus' name, I want this gift—but only if it's from You. Please protect me if it's not from You."

Several women gathered around, then laid their hands on me. As they prayed, I felt ill at ease, as if an evil presence had entered our small group. So I intensified my silent prayer for protection. Then, suddenly, out of the dark, a bright light appeared, shining like the noonday sun right onto my face, and my eyes felt riveted to it. Within that light a pure white dove appeared, fluttering its wings. But something was wrong: half of the dove was black! When I (mentally) asked God what it meant, I heard a gentle, but firm voice say, "Truth and error are mixed together in this place. Be careful."

In deep thought, I quietly left the circle of women and walked out of the meeting into the moonlit mountain night, where the stars looked close enough to touch. What I'd experienced surrounded me with solemn awe and wonder, and I've kept that incident close to my heart ever since.

The next morning at breakfast, I noticed the pastor staring at me. Then he asked, "What happened to you last night? I know something happened. I could see it!"

Too timid in those days to speak much, I didn't reply. I simply glanced at him for a moment, then calmly walked back to my room, asked a friend to help me get down the mountain, gathered my few belongings, then left. Although I admired those sincere, selfless

Christians for their ministry to orphans, I realized that my young faith had been seriously challenged by their well-meaning efforts to teach me. But I left secure in the belief that the Bible, and the Bible only, was the sole authority for my faith and doctrine.

Emerging from my reverie, I saw that the pastor had arrived at the riverside and was wading out into the calm current. I then turned my attention back to the young people who would soon be immersed, one by one, in those now gentle waters of the Moei.

I couldn't help but send silent, hope-filled petitions to Heaven for each of those special baptismal candidates, that the Holy Spirit would be their Guide from that day forward. I prayed also that every one of those young people would always stay true to the Bible as their sole authority all the way along their individual faith journeys.

# # # # #

EPILOGUE
By Paula Montgomery

In the spring of 2018, after returning to the U.S. on another furlough, Lena Adams stayed at my Pacific Northwest home for five fabulous days. The two of us literally combed through the "pages of her life," a manuscript she had worked on for years, so I could learn more and begin the creative process of re-writing her story. Thankfully, email closed the gap between my side of the planet and hers in Thailand, allowing us to continue communicating.

Today, Lena and Paul still live among the lime trees at Sunshine Orchard Learning Center. The couple's current sixteen Karen children all happily inhabit their home, where Lena still cooks on a two-burner propane stove for their sizable family and frequent visitors. Although their grown American-born son Josiah has moved across the road, he is still very much a part of their ministry, enhancing that ministry with his photographic and technical talents.

With hundreds of students (and twelve grades now) having outgrown the six-room school building, more classrooms are urgently needed. Sadly, the old vocational building became a safety hazard because of extensive termite damage and had to be torn down. Therefore, additional classrooms are now necessary for vocational training in weaving, sewing, home economics, mechanics, etc.

Across the road, the school's staff houses, constructed in the same Thai style as the Adams' home, are scattered throughout the beautiful river property, some nestled in woods, and others overlooking ponds. Nearby are dormitories and the chapel. But additional classrooms are needed on this property as well, along with more housing for staff and volunteers.

Sunshine Orchard Learning Center, its three branch mountain mission schools, and the Adams' dream-come-true, their own children's home, all depend solely on donations—and buckets of faith—from month to month and, sometimes, day to day.

Lena is especially fond of the biblical book of Isaiah, so I will describe Sunshine Orchard and its wide ministry with a fitting quote from that ancient prophet in the International Children's Bible: *You should feed those who are hungry. You should take care of the needs of those who are troubled. Then your light will shine in the darkness. And you will be bright like sunshine at noon* (Isaiah 58:10).

Over more than a decade, many students have been baptized, have graduated from Sunshine Orchard Learning Center, and are now carrying "The Light of the World" to the "darkness" around them.

To sign up for Sunshine Orchard's newsletter,
see its website: www.karenoutreach.org
For more information or to donate to their non-profit ministry:
www.shathal.org
or donate by mail:
Shathal, P.O. Box 7803, Kalispell, MT 59904

LENA'S ADDENDUM

I'll forever be grateful to Paula Montgomery for her incredible dedication and painstaking work over the past few years, crafting sections of my story into a publishable manuscript. She not only used her expertise as the author of eleven inspiring books, but she also sorted through my experiences and brought just the right events back to life. Now others will learn that God still works miracles today! It's my earnest desire for readers to gain a deeper faith in His personal love for them. I hope, too, that at least some of those readers will echo Isaiah's words from many centuries ago, *Then I heard the voice of the Lord, saying, "Whom shall I send, and who will go for Us?" Then I said, "Here am I. Send me!"* (See Isaiah 6:8 NASB.)